SIGNS OF THE JUDGEMENT, ONOMASTICA SACRA AND THE GENERATIONS FROM ADAM

University of Pennsylvania
Armenian Texts and Studies

Supported by the Sarkes Tarzian Fund

Editor
Michael E. Stone

Number 3

SIGNS OF THE JUDGEMENT, ONOMASTICA SACRA AND THE GENERATIONS FROM ADAM

SIGNS OF THE JUDGEMENT, ONOMASTICA SACRA AND THE GENERATIONS FROM ADAM

by
Michael E. Stone

SCHOLARS PRESS

Distributed by
Scholars Press
PO Box 2268
101 Salem St.
Chico, CA. 95927

SIGNS OF THE JUDGEMENT, ONOMASTICA SACRA AND THE GENERATIONS FROM ADAM

by

Michael E. Stone

Library of Congress Cataloging in Publication Data
Main entry under title:

Signs of the judgement, Onomastica sacra, and The
    generations from Adam.

    (University of Pennsylvania Armenian texts and
studies ; no. 3)
    Latin,   Armenian,   and   Hebrew   texts,   with
accompanying English translation for the latter two.
    Includes bibliographical references and indexes.
    1.   Judgement   Day.   2.   Bible—Names.   3.
Bible—Chronology. 4. Bible—Genealogy. I. Stone, Michael
E., 1938-   . II. Series: Pennsylvania. University.
University of Pennsylvania Armenian texts and studies ;
no. 3.
BT880.S56   236'.9   80-28371

ISBN 0-89130-460-6
ISBN 0-89130-461-4 (pbk.)

Printed in the United States of America

1   2   3   4   5

Edwards Brothers, Inc.
Ann Arbor, Michigan 48104

Dedicated to

GERSHOM G. SCHOLEM

whose learning and understanding have
guided and inspired me.

TABLE OF CONTENTS

The four writings published in this volume share
two traits. The first is the diversity of their character. In the course of arranging the texts planned for
inclusion in other volumes of Armenian pseudepigraphical
texts, it became apparent that certain documents fitted
naturally into none of them. Yet they were of inherent
interest and it was therefore decided to gather them in
a volume of their own, a volume to be typified by the
variety of the documents which comprise it.

The second trait, perhaps a correlative of the
first, is that not all of these texts are of the exact
types usually included in collections of "Apocrypha and
Pseudepigrapha". Indeed, in recent years it has come to
be recognized that the body of so-called pseudepigrapha
is not a fixed canon. To the contrary, it has become
broadened and extended to comprehend a wide range of
earlier and later crystallizations of traditions concerning biblical texts, personalities, and events. [1]
Moreover, the study of the Armenian pseudepigrapha must
properly include texts which are important for the
understanding of the development of these biblical traditions among the Armenians.

These observations are particularly relevant to two
of the documents published here, Onomastica Sacra Armeniaca and The Generations of Adam. They clearly apper-

1. On terminology see: A.-M Denis, Introduction aux
Pseudepigraphes grecs de l'A.T. (Studia in Veteris
Testamenti Pseudepigrapha, I), Leiden 1970, p. xi.
A clear example of this extended use of the term is
evident in the range of works included in the Pseude-
pigrapha Series of Texts and Translations. See most
recently J. H. Charlesworth, The Pseudepigrapha and
Modern Research (SCS 7;Missoula, S.P. 1976) 17,28.

tain to the development of biblical traditions, but are
not formally of the type usually included under the ru-
bric "Apocrypha and Pseudepigrapha". Their position in
the present volume, nonetheless, flows clearly from the
considerations set forth above.

The other two works, The Signs of the Judgement and
The Peoples of the Sons of Noah are of more familiar
types and their affiliation of the Apocrypha and Pseudepigrapha is immediately evident.

The four documents are of varying degrees of interest, and their chief characteristics are set forth in
the "Introductory Remarks". In the case of one, The
Signs of Judgement, its existence in various European
tongues and the discovery of a previously unrecognized
Hebrew translation, as well as its great intrinsic interest, required a particularly extensive discussion.
Another, Onomastica Sacra Armeniaca, is extant in so
many manuscripts and types that it was feasible to publish only part of them in full.

The various texts from Armenian manuscripts in the
Library of the Armenian Patriarchate in Jerusalem, the
Library of the Mechitarist Fathers in Venice, the Bibliothèque Nationale in Paris and the Matenadaran in Erevan
are published by permission of the Librarians of those
centers of learning. The Hebrew text from Bodl. MS.Heb.
d 11 (fol. 257r and v) is published by permission of
the Keeper of Oriental Books, the Bodleian Library.

The author is particularly indebted to the judic-
ious and learned counsel and unfailing encouragement of
Archbishop Norayr Bogharian, Librarian of Manuscripts of
the Armenian Patriarchate in Jerusalem.

The Israel Academy of Science and Humanities, the
Research Funds of the Hebrew University of Jerusalem and
the Tarzian Chair of Armenian History and Culture of the
University of Pennsylvania have all proffered material
support in the preparation of this book.

Michael E. Stone   Jerusalem, 1980

MANUSCRIPTS PUBLISHED HERE FOR THE FIRST TIME

ARMENIAN

Erevan

No. 533, p. 234	Sons of Noah	1660
No. 2261, fols. 300v ff.	Onomastica	XVII century
No. 8076, fols. 221r–222r	Generations of Adam	XVII century

Jerusalem

No. 657, fols. 285r ff.	Onomastica	no date
No. 857, fols. 101r ff.	Onomastica	no date
No. 1008, fols. 1 r ff.	Onomastica	no date
No. 1173, fols. 3r ff.	Onomastica	XVII century
No. 1352, pp. 297 ff.	Onomastica	1688
No. 1372, pp. 29 ff.	Onomastica	no date
No. 1422, fols. 325r ff.	Onomastica	XVII century
No. 1448, fols. 263r ff.	Onomastica	1583
No. 1666, fols. 97r ff.	Onomastica	1642
No. 1672, fols. 5 ff.	Onomastica	XVII century
No. 1682, fols. 185 ff.	Onomastica	1359
No. 1699, pp. 10 ff.	Onomastica	XVII century
No. 1912, pp. 7 ff.	Onomastica	no date
No. 2481, pp. 123 ff.	Onomastica	XIII century

Paris, Bibliothèque Nationale

Cod, Arm. 140 fols. 239v ff.	Onomastica	no date

Venice, Mechitarist Fathers

No. 39,   pp. 120 ff.   Onomastica   no date

No. 544,   pp. 1 ff.   Onomastica   XVI-XVII centuries

No. 1409, pp. 1 ff.   Onomastica   no date

HEBREW

Oxford, Bodleian Library

Cod. Heb d 11   fols. 257r-257v The Signs XIV century

TRANSCRIPTION OF THE ARMENIAN ALPHABET

Աա	Բբ	Գգ	Դդ	Եե	Զq	Էէ	Ըը	Թթ	Ժժ	Իի
A	B	G	D	E	Z	Ē	Ě	T'	Ž	I

Լլ	Խխ	Ծծ	Կկ	Հհ	Ձձ	Ղղ	Ճճ	Մմ	Յյ	Նն
L	X	C	K	H	J	Ł	Č	M	Y	N

Շշ	Ոո	Չչ	Պպ	Ջջ	Ռռ	Սս	Վվ	Տտ	Րր	Ցց
Š	O	Č'	P	J̌	Ṙ	S	V	T	R	C'

Ււ	Փփ	Քք	Oo	Ֆֆ
W	P'	K'	Ō	F

BIBLIOGRAPHICAL ABBREVIATIONS

Aleppo Catalogue

    A. Surmēyan, Catalogue des manuscrits armeniens
se trouvant a Alep a l'Eglise des Quarante Martyrs, Jerusalem: St. James Press, 1935(Armenian)

Amalyan   H.M. Amalyan, Mediaeval Armenian Glossaries
(5th-15th centuries), Erevan: Academy of
Sciences, 1966 (Armenian).

Ap. Elijah

    J.M. Rosenstiehl, L'Apocalypse d'Elie (Textes
et Etudes pour ... judaisme intertestamentaire,
1), Paris: Geuthner, 1972.

Apocalypse of Thomas

    M.R. James, The Apocryphal New Testament,
Oxford: 1955, pp. 555-562.

Arm. 4 Ezra

    M.E. Stone, The Armenian Version of 4 Ezra
(Pennsylvania Armenian Texts and Studies, 1)
Missoula: Scholars Press, 1978.

Berlin Catalogue

    N. Karamianz, Verzeichniss der armenischen Hand-
schriften der koeniglichen Bibliothek zu Berlin,
Berlin: Asher, 1888.

Bodleian Catalogue

    S. Baronian & F.C. Conybeare, Catalogue of the
Armenian Manuscripts in the Bodleian Library,
Oxford: 1918.

Book of John the Evangelist

    M.R. James, The Apocryphal New Testament,
Oxford: 1955, pp. 181-193.

Bousset, Antichrist
        W. Bousset, The Antichrist Legend, tr. A.H.
        Keane, London: Hutchinson, 1896.

British Library Catalogue
        F.C. Conybeare, Catalogue of the Armenian Manu-
        scripts in the British Museum, London: British
        Museum, 1913.

Bzommar Catalogue
        M. Keschischian, Katalog der armenischen Hand-
        schriften in der Bibliothek des Klosters Bzommar,
        1-2, Vienna: Mechitarist Press, 1964, 1971
        (Armenian).

Erevan Catalogue
        Ō.Eganyan, A. Zeyt'unyan and P'. Ant'abyan,
        Catalogue of the Manuscripts of the Mastoc'
        Library, 1-2, Erevan: Academy of Sciences, 1965,
        1970 (Armenian).

Even-Shmuel
        Y. Even-Shmuel, Midreshei Geulah, Tel-Aviv:
        Mosad Bialik, 1943 (Hebrew).

Galata Catalogue
        Babken Catholicos, Catalogue of the Manuscripts
        of the Armenian National Library of Galatia,
        Antelias: Catholicossate of Sis, 1961 (Armenian).

Geniza Daniel Apocalypse
        Y. Even-Shmuel, Midreshei Geulah, Tel-Aviv:
        Mosad Bialik, 1943, pp. 249-252.

Heist   W.W. Heist, The Fifteen Signs before Doomsday
        East Lansing: Michigan State College, 1952.

James, Apoc. N.T.
        M.R. James, The Apocryphal New Testament,
        Oxford: 1955.

Jellinek, B.M.
        A. Jellinek, Bet Ha-Midrasch, 1-6, 3ed;
        Jerusalem: Wahrmann, 1967 (Hebrew).

Jerusalem Catalogue
        N. Bogharian, Grand Catalogue of St. James Manu-
        scripts, 1-6, Jerusalem: St. James Press, 1968-
        1976 (Armenian).

Kurdian Catalogue
        Armenian Manuscripts : Catalogue of an Exhibi-
        tion at the University of Kansas Library,
        Kansas: 1955.

Ladder of Jacob
        M.R. James, Lost Apocrypha of the Old Testament,
        London: S.P.C.K., 1920, pp. 96-103.

Last Vision of Daniel
        A. Vassiliev, Anecdota Graeco-Byzantina, 1,
        Moscow: 1893,

New Julfa Catalogue
        S. Ter Avetissian, Katalog der armenischen Hand-
        schriften in der Bibliothek des Klosters in Neu-
        Djoulfa, Vienna: Mechitarist Press, 1970
        (Armenian).

P.G.   J. Migne (ed.) Patrologia Graeca, 1-161, Paris:
         Migne, 1844-1902.

P.L.   J. Migne (ed), Patrologia Latina, 1-221, Paris:
         Migne, 1844-1904.

Paris Catalogue
        F. Macler, Catalogue des manuscrits arméniens
        et georgiens de la Bibliothèque Nationale,
        Paris: Bibliotheque Nationale, 1908.

Pauly-Wissowa
        A.F. von Pauly and G. Wissowa, Real-encyclopadie
        der classischen altertums Wissenschaft, 1-24,
        Stuttgart: Metzler, 1893-1963.

Sefer Eliyyahu

> Y. Even-Shmuel, Midreshei Geulah, Tel-Aviv:
> Mosad Bialik, 1943, pp. 41-48.

Seventh Vision of Daniel

> G. Kalemkiar, Die siebente Vision Daniels,
> Vienna: Mechitarist Press, 1892.

Tabriz Catalogue

> H. Adjarian, Katalog der armenischen Hand-
> schriften in Taebriz, Vienna: Mechitarist Press,
> 1910 (Armenian).

Vienna Catalogue

> H. Oskian, Katalog der armenischen Handschriften
> in der Mechitaristen-Bibliothek zu Wien, 2,
> Vienna: Mechitarist Press, 1963 (Armenian).

Wutz   F.X. Wutz, Onomastica Sacra (Texte und Unter-
            suchungen, 41), Leipzig: Hinrichs, 1915.

SIGNS

/	end of line or page in manuscript
	lacuna in manuscript
˙	(over letter) partly legible only
. . .	(on line) words lost by the textual tradition
< >	material introduced from another source
⌐ ¬	uncorrected corruption
{ }	material introduced from a correction or note in the manuscript by a second hand
∿	order of words reversed
+	adds
$1°$, $2°$	(following letter of word) first, second, etc. occurrence of letter in word or word in verse
A^*	text as originally written by scribe
A^0	text as corrected by original scribe
A^1, A^2	f rst, second, etc. corrector (not scribe)
A^c	corrector other than scribe

OTHER ABBREVIATIONS

above	written above
col(s)	column(s)
cor	corrected, corrector
corr.for	corrupt for
dittog	dittography
eras	erasure, erased
f., ff.	following
fol(s)	folio(s)
haplgr	haplography
hmarkt	homoeoarchton
hmt	homoeoteleuton
illeg	illegible
inc	beginning
ln(s)	line(s)
let	letter
marg	margin
MS	manuscript
n	note
om	omit
omn	all witnesses
r	recto
rel	all witnesses except those cited by siglum
rep.	reprint
s.v.	(in Index to Onomastica) spelling variant
tantum	only as much text in this unit survives as is cited
tot	totally
v	verso
V(L)L	variant reading(s)
vs(s)	verse(s)

All further abbreviations follow the list in <u>JBL</u> 95 (1976) 334-346.

PART ONE

THE SIGNS OF THE JUDGEMENT

Introductory Remarks

The text which we have entitled The Signs of the Judgement is extant in very numerous versions in European languages.[1] The Armenian versions were first printed a few years ago, but their relationship to the widespread medieval European texts has not been recognized nor have they been translated into any modern language. The Armenian texts are unique in that they are the first oriental version of this material known. In an appendix, a Hebrew version of the work is published here for the first time, together with some critical comments.

The Manuscripts and Editions

The Armenian version was published in two diplomatic printings in 1972 by Bishop Norair Bogharian in his Grand Catalogue of St. James Manuscripts. These two texts were based on manuscripts in Jerusalem, so designated below:

I Jerusalem, No. 1729, Miscellany copied in the monastery of Lim in 1741 C.E., p. 320 (Jerusalem Catalogue, 6.40–42);

II Jerusalem, No. 1861, Miscellany copied in New Julfa (Isfahan) in 1669 C.E., p. 135 (Jerusalem Catalogue, 6.248–254).

These two texts are printed and translated synoptically, and the material in which they differ from one another is italicized.

For the sake of comparison, two Latin versions are presented: B–that attributed (falsely) to the Venerable Bede, probably stemming from the eleventh or twelfth century (Patrologia Latina 94.555):[2] and C – that included in the Historia Scholastica of Peter Comestor

(d. 1179 C.E.; Patrologia Latina 198.1611). A third,
associated Latin version, the oldest form of which
occurs in Peter Damien's De novissimis et Antichristo
(Patrologia Latina 145.840-842) is less closely related
to these two texts and not given here in full.

The Hebrew version occurs in the unique manuscript
of the Chronicle of Jerahmeel which is preserved in the
Bodleian Library in Oxford.[3] The manuscript is Bodleian
MS Hebrew d.11, copied by R. Eleazar b. Asher haLevi in
the fourteenth century in the Rhineland.[4] The text
occurs on fols. 257r - 257v. The last third of the
preceding page has been left blank and the text is
provided with its own title which states that it was
drawn from the Book of Jerahmeel. It is followed by
a Hebrew translation of Pseudo-Philo, Liber Antiquita-
tum Biblicarum 10:3 ff. This material is integrated into
the end of the text of The Signs of the Judgement and,
as it stands, forms a natural continuation of it. The
ink of the manuscript is rubbed at a number of places
on fol. 257r, but all the readings are certain, based
on autopsy examination.

Versions in European Languages

In his study of the legend of The Fifteen Signs of
the Doomsday, W. W. Heist reached certain conclusions
about the origins and growth of this material. Drawing
upon the various versions of the Apocalypse of Thomas,
its earliest form is that found in the Old Irish Saltair
na Rann (tenth century) with another Old Irish work of
the same date, The Evernew Tongue, being a separate,
less important source.[5] The seven subsequent types and
further subtypes which Heist discerns among the more
than eighty versions of this material which he examined
are naturally complex in their composition. A number of
them, including those of pseudo-Bede, Comestor, and
Damien know the attribution to Jerome who supposedly

drew upon <u>Annales</u> <u>Hebraeorum</u> (p. 196).

    Furthermore, by his analysis, Heist discovers that
additional native Irish versions existed, close to but
independent of pseudo-Bede.[6] This, he argues, suggests
that the origin of <u>The</u> <u>Signs</u> is to be sought in Ireland,[7]
and that this material probably reached its present
state in the eleventh or twelfth century.

    The Armenian version clearly belongs to the same
branch of the stemma as pseudo-Bede, Comestor and Dami-
en, but it is not identical with any single one of them.
The meaning of the existence of this version is explored
below; it may conceivably indicate that, in spite of
Heist's analysis, an earlier stage of this text should
be posited. The position of the Hebrew version among
the medieval European language witnesses is unclear.
It is indubitably of a different type to the Armenian
version and to those Latin texts here considered, even
though it is a translation from Latin.

    The origins of the various separate signs in earli-
er sources are dealt with very briefly by Heist, <u>passim</u>.
In the Commentary we have been concerned chiefly with
problems of the Armenian version but, in order to indicate the broad spectrum of sources which <u>The</u> <u>Signs</u> and
its immediate ancestors are utilizing, chief parallels
in ancient sources are noted.

<u>The</u> <u>Character</u> and <u>Relationships</u> <u>of</u> <u>the</u>
<u>Armenian</u> <u>and</u> <u>Hebrew</u> <u>Versions</u>

    The Armenian version is written in good classical
Armenian. In II a number of Christian elements may be
observed, notably in the framework within which the text
is presented. All of these are missing from I.[8] Moreover, the formulation of the conclusion in II, with its
reference to St. Gregory and the Pit, indicates the
peculiarly Armenian character of this Christian framework. In contrast, in I the text is attributed to a

Jewish source and the significance of this will be
discussed below. Although in I the order of Days XIV
and XV has been reversed, in general this recension
finds corroboration in pseudo-Bede and Comestor in
those cases in which it differs from II. Furthermore,
certain indications of a grammatical type show that
recension II is later in language than recension I.
It is also longer in some places and varies in others.
At one point where II has a lacuna, I preserves the
complete text (Day X).

From a literary examination, the relationship
between the recensions emerges more clearly. It seems
likely that I is more original, for no reason can be
imagined for the rejection of the framework (i.e., the
superscription and the conclusion) of II and its replace-
ment with that of I. On the other hand, reverence for
a national saint does provide an easily understood
motive, so the peculiarly Armenian character of the
framework of II is a clear indication of its secondary
character. Moreover, the framework of recension II
invokes scriptural authority for the signs, yet in the
list of signs itself no verses are alluded to. That
such could have been found is clear from the Latin text
of Peter Comestor who cites verses in his concluding
observations, as well as from the biblicizing recension
of the Hebrew version. This is another indication of
the secondary character of the framework.

In the Table below, the relationship between I, II,
B, and C emerges. First, Armenian and Latin B C represent two independent but closely related forms of the
textual tradition of The Signs. There are numerous cases
in which I and II agree against the reading of B and C.
Some of these are: Superscription, both Latin versions
are attributed to Jerome; Day I, both Armenian versions
add that the purpose of the flood is to show that God
can destroy the earth; Day IX, (Day XIII of B), the

the bones of the dead act in an identical fashion in
both Latin texts, different from Armenian; Day XIII,
(XIV of B), the purpose of the death of all men (so as
to be able to rise in the subsequent resurrection) is
given by Latin, but lacks in both Armenian witnesses.

Second, it may be easily observed from a comparison
of I with II that there are many cases in which II is
longer than I. In virtually none of these cases does
the reading of II find corroboration in Latin B or C.
Such are: Day I, "according to the measure of the
Flood"; Day II, "of the dry land --- be seen"; Day III,
"perish", "sand", "loudly --- stink"; Day IV, "and dry
up"; Day VI, "Mountains and", "with a --- destroyed".
Certain other instances of readings of II against I find
no resolution in Latin B or C. In no case is a clear
agreement between II and Latin B or C against the reading of I to be observed. A marginal exception is Day
III "pisces et" B II; omit C I. This reading is also
conflationary with those listed above.

Third, in Latin B a measure of dislocation of the
order of the text has taken place, particularly the
omission from it of the text of Day XV found in the
other versions. This may be a result of a textual
process (perhaps homoeoteleuton novissima --- nova).

In spite of that, the actual text of B, where it is
extant, has many readings in common with Armenian,
against the readings of C. Such are: Day I, "in loco
suo" C (omit B I II); Day II, "ad ima" B I II (omit C);
Day V "omnes" B I II (omit C); Day IX, "omnes--conver-
tentur" B I II ("aequabitur terra" C); Day XII "de caelo"
B I II (omit C); Day XIII, "omnes homines" B I II
("viventes" C). This indicates that, although the
order of events in B is secondary, its text is important.

Fourth, there are a number of instances in which C
agrees with Armenian, against the reading of B. Such are:

Day VI, "collidentur" C I II ("debellabunt" B); "et
unaquaeque" -- fin B (omit C I II); Day VII, "mare" C I II
(omit B), "ab ortu --- occasum" B (omit C I II); Day
VIII "generalis" C I II ("qualis --- mundi" B); Day IX,
"et erit --- terrae" B (omit C I II). From these last
two groups of examples it follows that neither B nor C
shows a special relationship to Armenian.

TABLE

Armenian   Latin

Day	I	II	B	C
I	Flood of 40 cubits, like a wall to show that God can destroy the earth		Flood of 40 cubits like a wall	
II	Sea dries up to the depths, scarcely seen	Sea dries up to depths of dry land and water not seen	Sea descends to depths whose summit is scarcely to be seen III They will be in balance as originally	Sea descends so as to be just seen
III	Whales upon water cry out to heaven	Fish and whales upon sand perish, cry out, smell	IV Fish and marine beasts upon water cry out, meaning known only to God	Marine beast upon seas cry out to heaven
IV	Plants and shoots drip bloody dew	Trees and all plants drip bloody dew and wither up	V Waters burn to west (see Arm VII) VI All plants and trees give bloody dew	Sea and waters burn
V	All buildings destroyed		VII All buildings destroyed	Plants and trees give bloody dew

	Armenian		Latin	
Day	I	II	B	C
VI	Rocks smite one another	Mountains and rocks smite one another with a terrible noise and are destroyed	VIII Rocks fight one another, are divided into three parts and each smites the other	Buildings destroyed
VII	Sea and earth are burnt with fire (see B V)			Rocks smite one another
VIII	General earthquake		IX Earthquake un-paralleled since creation	General earthquake
IX	Levelling of mountains and valleys		X All hills and valleys become plain	Levelling of earth
X	Men in caverns come forth, are as mad, unable to talk to each other	Men [lacuna]	XI Men come forth from caverns, run as mad, unable to reply to one another	Men come forth from caves, go as mad, unable to talk to one another
XI	Dead go out of graves	Dead fall out of graves	(See XIII below)	Bones of dead rise and stand on graves
XII	Stars appear to fall from heaven		Stars and signs fall from heaven	Stars fall
			XIII Bones of dead gathered and rise up to graves (see rel.XI)	

Armenian

Latin

Day	I	II	B	C
XIII	All men die		XIV All men die so as to rise with the dead	All men die so as to rise with the dead
XIV	XV Heavens and earth burn	Heavens and ear-h burn	XV Heavens and earth burn up to the end of hell	Heaven and earth burn
XV	XIV New heavens and earth	New heavens and earth		New heavens and earth

The Hebrew version which has not been included in the above comparison, is a representative of a text type showing characteristics independent of both the Latin and the Armenian texts. It contains an extensive introduction and a long conclusion not found elsewhere. Certain of the signs are quite different (e.g., Day VI) or formulated very differently (e.g., Day X). Moreover, the Hebrew version is characterized by a biblicizing tendency. In numerous cases it has introduced a clear biblical reference either by reformulation or by addition. It may be of interest to observe that the following chief biblical references are made: 2 Sam 22:8 (Day VIII); Ezek 38:20 (Day IX) Isa 2:19,21 (Day X); Jer 22:19 (Day XI); Isa 51:6, 34:4 (Day XII);Dan 12:3 (Day XIII). Of these, only the reference in Day X is to be discerned clearly in the Armenian and Latin B C versions. In the introductory paragraphs Isa 46:16 is quoted. In the text of Day XV which is integrated into the following conclusion, four quotations are strung together: Dan 12:2-3, Judg 5:31, Isa 52:8, and Joel 4:12.

This version was apparently translated into Hebrew from a classical language, probably Latin. This is indicated by the following considerations: First, the introduction contains a classical (or rather a late classical) legend about Mt. Olympus and the calculation of the Olympiads. This legend has a tenuous connection with the text as it is now preserved, being tied in by the common interest in the highest mountain. The sentence at the actual point of juncture is incomplete, which perhaps accounts for this apparent tenuousness. Yet its very inclusion clearly indicates the character of the Vorlage of the Hebrew version. The tradition that Mount Olympus is higher than any other mountain and therefore is not afflicted by the winds is to be

found in the writings of Isidore of Seville. He states:
mons Olympus in ea est qui excellenti vertice tantus
adtollitur ut in cacumine eius nec nubes nec venti
sentiantur (Etymolog. XIV.4.13).[9] No clear parallel
to the part of the story here which speaks of the
writing of the names of the Olympic victors in the soft
earth at the peak of Mt. Olympus has been found, but
there seems to be no reason to doubt its Greek or Latin
origins.

Second, the fact that this text is bound together
with the translation from Pseudo-Philo which follows it,
is indicative, but of course not conclusive of this
origin. Third, the text of The Signs of the Judgement
contains a transliterated Latin word, balaenas (Day III).
Incidentally, this is not the word found in the corresponding place in B and C. This is not surprising for
the Latin recension behind the Hebrew version was very
different from these texts. From the above considerations, however, it may firmly be concluded that this
version was translated into Hebrew from Latin.

This indicates that this Hebrew version cannot be
a form of some original from which the extant Latin and
Armenian versions were made. Such importance as it has
lies in the fact that it is a translation of a Latin
text of a type different from B and C. It seems difficult to determine whether the biblicizing reworking was
the handiwork of the translator, who incidentally wrote
a very literate and pleasing Hebrew, or of the Latin
version which he was rendering.

Attribution to a Jewish Source

Armenian I and both Latin versions are attributed
to a Jewish original. The Christianization of Armenian
II, as indicated above, is specifically Armenian in
character and is limited to the framework, not penetra-
ting to the body of the text of The Signs proper. [10]

A title similar to that of I may be observed at the
head of an Armenian text which turns out to be an
extract from the Babylonian Talmud. The exact formulation of that superscription is Եբրայեցի Գրոց՛ն զատք
"We have found in Hebrew books."[11] This parallel lends
a certain prima facie credibility to the statement made
by I, since it shows that translations of Jewish books
were preserved in Armenian and were provided with accurate attribution.[12] Both Latin texts state that the
work is found in annalibus Hebraeorum which shows a
tradition identical with Armenian.

If, however, the thesis of Heist as to the deriva-
tion of this text from a body of material combining
tenth century Old Irish writings and forms of the Latin
version of the Apocalypse of Thomas is correct, then the
origins of the attribution to Jerome as well as to the
Annales Hebraeorum remain puzzling, as he observes. [13]
This mention of the Annales Hebraeorum may explain the
attribution to the famed Hebraist - Jerome, but why the
work, if it was composed in Ireland in the eleventh
century, should be given a fictitious Jewish source is
obscure.

The question of the original language of the Armenian version remains without solution. It is improbable
that Armenian is original, although doubtless the framework of II was composed in Armenian. Whether its original was Latin or Greek or another language cannot be
determined on any objective grounds that could be
discerned by the present writer. Heist's theories
would demand an eleventh century date at the earliest,
and presumably a Latin Vorlage.

Although it thus seems likely that the document is
of Christian origin, it remains notable that the text
itself contains no clearly Christian elements, nor is
any of the portents listed necessarily drawn from the
New Testament. Admittedly, some of them are paralleled

in later Christian sources alone but granted the highly
conservative, traditional nature of these signs, indeed
of much of what is contained in the literature on these
and related topics, as well as the possibility or even
probability of mutual influence, it will readily be
conceded that the Christian character of a single sign
or of the pattern of occurrence of a number of signs
must be very distinctive indeed to serve as sole and
conclusive proof of a Christian origin.[14] Mere occurrence in a Christian apocalypse is not enough.

The discovery of an Armenian version which has
undergone certain textual development in that language
may serve to open up the issue of origins once more.
It could, of course, be a translation from Latin,
depending ultimately on Old Irish sources. Perhaps,
however, the filiation suggested by Heist should take
clearer account of the possible origins of a list of
fifteen signs in older writings, parallel to his suggested Irish source documents. This would not be out
of keeping with the unique role of Ireland in preserv-
ing ancient texts little known elsewhere in Europe.[15]

The Character of the Document

The text is a schematic enumeration of the signs
and portents which are to occur during a period of fifteen days preceding the Last Judgement. The idea that
various upheavals of nature and its order are to precede
the eschaton is an ancient one indeed. It may already
be observed in the Jewish literature of the period of
the Second Temple, which in its turn draws upon more
antique sources in the Bible.[16] One of the salient
points in which The Signs of the Judgement appears
to be unusual when compared with the sources of that
era is in the precise distribution of these events over
a designated period of fifteen days.

The idea that these portents, the "Messianic Woes" as they may be called, were divided into parts is to be found in 2 Apoc. Bar. 27 which refers to twelve parts. This text, stemming from a work composed soon after the end of the first century C.E., is very like another document, a Baraitha which has been preserved in the Babylonian Talmud, Sanhedrin, fol. 97a. In this, a week of years at the close of which the Messiah will come is described and the events which will take place in each year adnumbrated. In both of these documents, the actual events which will take place in each "part" or "year" bear little resemblance to those in The Signs.[17]

An even closer parallel to our text is to be found in The Apocalypse of Thomas suggested by Heist to be an indirect source of The Signs. Here a week of days is delineated, which are "the seven signs (before) the ending of the world".[18] The events of each day are set forth, attributed to a given hour of the day.[19]

As in the two cases mentioned in the last paragraph the actual events, except for one or two very commonplace features, like earthquake, are very little like those of The Signs. The Apocalypse of Thomas is fairly ancient, being extant in a fifth-century fragment. In it, the week of days is mentioned, a measure of time standing in obvious relationship to the week of years in Sanhedrin, fol. 97a and in contrast with the fifteen days here.[20]

Structurally, in a final parallel to be noted, the strict timetable for the whole eschatological process, particularly in its more cataclysmic aspects, is to be observed in Sefer Eliyyahu. Due to the corruption of the dates in the extant manuscripts, it is quite difficult to discern the actual scheme of the chronology.[21]

The Signs appears to be rather inconsequent and to be composed of a series of traditional signs and portents and groups of such. Yet the relationship between

the individual signs and groups of signs has not been
adjusted or adapted to an overall conceptual structure.
This is a common literary feature of both Jewish and
Christian apocalypses, particularly of the later ones,
often a result of heavy dependence on earlier written
and oral sources.

The teaching of the document is typical of a pattern of apocalyptic eschatology which foresaw an increase of chaos and disorder in the world, presaging
the coming of the eschaton. In very many of the texts,
the chaos and disorder lead to or stem from the break-
down of the structure of human society.[22] In The Signs
of the Judgement the scope of the vision is cosmic; the
order of the cosmos will collapse and the sea, the earth,
the mountains, indeed the whole world will be subject to
a series of cataclysms. Consequently, the resolution
and renewal which are to follow the chaos will also be
of cosmic proportions.

The contrast of two ages is implied by this; the
time before the end is divided into fifteen measured
days which can be predicted in advance. The Signs of
the Judgement is thus based upon a view which teaches
a division of the times by a predetermined plan. The
predictions make quite explicit the very day upon which
each portent will happen. A somewhat similar chronological precision of predictions is to be observed in
the Baraitha in b. Sanhedrin fol. 97a. Like The Signs
of the Judgement that text discusses the actual units of
time. In the similar passage in 2 Apoc. Bar. 27, the
parts into which the events are divided are the subject
of discussion, not the exact days or years upon which
they will take place. The view expressed by the Baraitha in Sanhedrin, The Signs of the Judgement, and
Sefer Eliyyahu implies an extreme degree of historical
determinism.

It is appropriate to mention a few other peculiar-
ities of this text. The first is the very number fifteen, for which no rationale at all is apparent. This
contrasts with the Baraitha and the Apocalypse of Thomas
which have "a week" (i.e., of years) and highlights the
author's determinism as well as the vividness of his
imagination. Second, strangely, the text preserves no
hint of belief in an Anti-Christ or an Anti-Messiah such
as Armillos. This is a feature common to many of the
later apocalypses which the commentary shows to have
much in common with The Signs of the Judgement. Finally,
the text mentions no messiah or savior and no angels;
no cosmic or super-human protagonists figure in the
events. "Mythical" or "semi-mythical" features such
as frequently characterize the apocalypses, particularly
the later ones, are absent from this work.

Some remarks may be added on its place within the
Armenian tradition. The Armenians were rather interest-
ed in works of an apocalyptic character, often of the
type of those compositions of the Byzantine period which
were characterized by a wealth of circumstantial prediction, usually political in character. This is witnessed
by the abundance of such material composed or transmit-
ted in the Armenian language, including such writings as
The Seventh Vision of Daniel, The Vision of Enoch, The
Vision of Sahak, the Armenian additions to 4 Ezra and
a number of other works. A text like The Signs of the
Judgement doubtless seemed important to scribes and
thinkers preoccupied with this kind of speculation. It
would not be surprising to find that it, in its turn,
served as a source for some medieval Armenian apocalyp-
ticist.

1. Heist 23-34 outlines the material. He consulted
   eighty-nine versions of the legend, see pp. 204-
   212 for details. See also M. McNamara, The Apocrypha in the Irish Church (Dublin: Dublin Insti-
   tute Advanced Study, 1975) 128-132.

2. See Heist 96-7.

3. The existence of this version was brought to my
   attention by David Flusser who also kindly discussed it with me and made invaluable suggestions
   as to some of the readings and their interpretations.
   Part of the Chronicle of Jerahmeel was published in
   English translation by Moses Gaster, The Chronicles
   of Jerahmeel Or, The Hebrew Bible Historiale (London
   Royal Asiatic Society, 1899). The sections of the
   manuscript parallel to Pseudo-Philo, Liber Antiqui-
   tatum Biblicarum have been published by Daniel J.
   Harrington in Hebrew with a parallel English translation in The Hebrew Fragments of Pseudo-Philo
   (Texts and Translations 3; Pseudepigrapha Series 3;
   Missoula: SBL, 1974). His text does not contain the
   Hebrew version of the section of Bib. Ant. 10:3f.
   which follows The Signs of the Judgement in the
   manuscript as noted below.

4. On the manuscript see: A. Neubauer and A.E. Cowley,
   Catalogue of Hebrew Manuscripts in the Bodleian Lib-
   rary (Oxford: 1906) 2. cols. 209-215, esp. col. 213
   (MS No. 2797),

5. Heist passim and see conclusions, 193-195.

6. Ibid. 197-198.

7. Ibid. 195.

8. See in detail in the commentary on the superscription
   and the conclusion below.

9. The absence of meteorological phenomena on Mt. Olympus and the special quality of the air upon it are
   already noted in Odyssey VI, 41-45. That this is a
   function of its height is also the view of Augustine,
   Civ. Dei XV, 27. See in detail also: Pauly-Wissowa,

18, 1. 308-309.

10. See below, commentary on the superscription.

11. See: Michael E. Stone, "An Armenian Translation of a Baraitha in the Babylonian Talmud", HTR 68 (1970) 151-154

12. See also further comments in: Michael E. Stone, "Jewish Literature from the Period of the Second Temple in Armenian Literature", Lectures at the History Research Meetings, (Jerusalem; Israel Historical Society, 1973) 263-5 (Hebrew). This statement does not necessarily imply direct translation from Hebrew into Armenian.

13. Heist 108.

14. On these questions, see also: W. Bousset, Antichrist, passim.

15. Heist 201-202.

16. Convenient lists of sources are to be found in many books dealing with Jewish eschatology in the period of the Second Temple, and these sources will become evident in the course of the discussion of the parallels to the events listed in The Signs. See, by way of example: D. S. Russell, The Method and Message of Jewish Apocalyptic (Philadelphia: Fortress, 1964) 271-276 and the sources and bibliography there.

17. A comparison of the Baraitha and 2 Apoc. Bar. 27 may be found in: E.E. Urbach, The Sages: Their Concepts and Beliefs, (tr. I Abrahams; Jerusalem; Magnes, 1975) 676-678

18. The English is drawn from: M.R. James , Apoc N.T. 558-62.

19. No rationale seems evident for the choice of hours.

20. On the date of The Apocalypse of Thomas and other critical problems, see: E. Henneke and W. Schneemelcher, New Testament Apocrypha, tr. by R. McL.

Wilson (Philadelphia: Westminster, 1965) 2.798–800.
Further bibliography is to be found there.

21. Compare the textual material presented by M. But-
     tenweiser, Die hebräische Elias-Apokalypse
     (Leipzig: Pfeiffer, 1926) 16–26 and by Even-Shmuel
     39–48, 51–54, 374–379. The timetable of salvifica-
     tory events of Sefer Zerubbabel is also analogous
     to this material, ibid., pp. 71–88, 379–389.

22. The sources are manifold. See, for examples of
     one type of text: 4 Ezra 13:29 ff., Matt 24:7,
     m. Sot. 9:15, 1 Enoch 56:7, Melito, Pasch. Hom.
     51 ff., et al.

Եւ այլ վարդապետք ասեն
Թէ ընդերցաք ի գիրս Հրէից
որ լինելոց են Ժե նշան,
ի Ժե աւուրս յառաջ քան
զդատաստանն:

Վասն գալստեան Որդոյն
Աստուծոյ եւ կատարածի
աշխարհի, Թէ որպէս է
աՀեղ դատաստանն: Արդ մեք
որ ակն ունիմք գալստեանն
Քրիստոսի Աստուծոյ մերոյ,
վկայութեամբ Սուրբ Գրոց
եւ բանիւ առաքելոց եւ
մարգարէից եւ վկայութեամբ
Սուրբ Աւետարանին
Քրիստոսի որ այսպէս
լինելոց է աւերումն
աշխարհի ի վերջին ժամանակն,
Ժե նշան լինի յառաջ քան
զգալուստն Քրիստոսի.

I

And other doctors say, "We
have read in the books of
the Jews that there are going to be fifteen signs on
fifteen days before the
Judgement.

II

Concerning the coming of
the Son of God and the end
of the world, or in what
fashion is the terrible
Judgement. Now, we who
hope for the coming of
Christ our God, by the
witness of the Sacred
Scriptures, and by the
word of Apostles and
Prophets, and by the
witness of the holy
Gospel of Christ, (know)
that in this fashion is
the destruction of the
world going to be at the
last time. There are
fifteen signs before the
coming of Christ.

I   Առաջին օրն բարձրացի ծովն իւ կանգուն ի վերայ

բարձրագոյն լերանց   լերանց ըստ չափոյ

                                 Քրիստոսին

եւ կացցէ իբրեւ պարիսպ (զպարիսպ II) շուրջ զաշխարհաւս

ի նշան թէ կարող է   զի տեսցեն եւ զարմասցին

Աստուած տապալել զաշ-   եւ գիտասցեն թէ կարող է

խարհ որպէս հեղեղաւ :   Աստուած Քրիստեղեաւ

                                անցուցանել զաշխարհս :

II   Երկրորդ օրն իջցէ ծովն ի խոնարհ

մինչ հազիւ երեւեսցի :   զամաքի եւ այլ ոչ

                                երեւի քուր :

III   Երրորդ օրն կէտք մեծա-   Երրորդ օրն ձկունք եւ

մեծք ելեալ ի վերայ   կէտք մեծամեծք ելեալ

երեսաց քրոց գոչես-   տապալեն ի վերայ աւազոյ

ցեն մինչեւ լերկինս :   մեծաձայն գոչեսցեն

                                եւ մեռանեն եւ նեխեալ

                                հոտեցնեն զաշխարհս :

IV   Չորրորդ օրն տունկք   Չորրորդ օրն ծառք եւ

եւ բոյսք կաթեցու-   տունկք եւ ամենայն բոյսք

ցանեն գոդ արեան :   գոդ արեան կաթեցնեն եւ

                                չորանան :

V   Հինգերորդ օրն կործանեսցին (կործանին II) ամենայն

շինուածք :

I   On the first day the sea will rise forty cubits above

the highest mountains   the mountains according to

                                the measure of the Flood

and it will stand like a wall around the world

as a sign that God is   that they might see and

able to destroy the earth   wonder and know that God

as by a flood.   is able to make this earth

                                pass away through a flood.

II   On the second day the sea will go down to a depth

until it will be seen   of the dry land and no

with difficulty   more water will be seen.

III On the third day, very   On the third day, very

great whales, having   great fish and whales

come forth upon the   having come forth, perish

face of the waters, will   upon the sand. They will

cry up to the heavens.   cry loudly and die and,

                                having rotted will make

                                this world stink.

IV   On the fourth day   On the fourth day trees

plants and shoots shall   and plants and all shoots

drip dew of blood.   shall drip dew of blood

                                and dry up.

V   On the fifth day all buildings shall be (are II)

destroyed.

VI   *Վեցերորդ օրն վեմք*   *Վեցերորդ օրն լերինք եւ*
      հարկանիցեն ընդ   *վեմք հարկանեն ընդ*
      իրեարս: *իրարս ահագին թրնդմամբ*
                               եւ բլին:

VII   *Եօթներորդ օրն ծով եւ երկիր վառեցին հրով:*

VIII   *Ութերորդ օրն եղիցի ընդհանուր (ընթհանուր II) գետ-*
       նաշարժ:

IX   *Իններորդ օրն ամենայն լերինք եւ ձորք հաւասարեցին*
      (հաւասարեցեն II):

X   *Տասներորդ օրն, ելեալ մարդիկ*[23] *որ լինին ի յայրս*
     եւ ի խորշս երկրի, եւ շրջեցին որպէս խելագարեալս,
     եւ ոչ կարասցեն խօսել ընդ միմեանս:

XI   *Մետասաներորդ օրն ամե-*   *Մետասաներրորդ օրն ամե-*
      նայն մեռեալք արտաքս   *նայն մեռելնին արտաքս*
      գնան ի գերեզմանաց   *ի գերեզմանաց իւրեանց*
      իւրեանց: *անկանին:*

XII   *Երկոտասաներորդ օրն*   *Երկոտասաներորդ օրն*
       թուեցին աստեղ թէ   *թուեցեն աստեղ*
       անկեալ յերկնից: *անկանել յերկնից:*

XIII   *Երեքտասաներորդ օրն մեռանիցին (մեռանիցեն II) ամենայն*
       մարդիկ:

VI   On the sixth day rocks   On the sixth day <u>mountains</u>
     shall be smitten against   <u>and</u> rocks smite against
     one another.   one another <u>with</u> a <u>fear-</u>
                                  <u>full</u> <u>thundering</u> <u>and</u> <u>are</u>
                                  <u>destroyed</u>.

VII On the seventh day the sea and the earth will be
     burnt with fire.

VIII On the eighth day there will be a general earth-
     quake.

IX   On the ninth day all mountains and valleys will be
     leveled.

X   On the tenth day, men[23] who are in the caves and
     caverns (or: holes) of the ground having come forth,
     they will go around like madmen and will be unable
     to speak with one another.

XI   On the eleventh day all   On the eleventh day all
     <u>the</u> <u>dead</u> <u>come</u> outside   die. <u>They</u> <u>fall</u> outside
     their graves.   their graves.

XII On the twelfth day stars   On the twelfth day stars
     shall appear <u>to</u> <u>have</u>   shall appear
     <u>fallen</u> from heaven.   <u>to</u> <u>fall</u> from heaven.

XIII On the thirteenth day, all men shall die.

23   II omits the text from մարդիկ to the end of the
     tenth day.

XV Հնգետասաներորդ օրն XIV Չորեքտասաներորդ օրն
    վառեցին երկինք եւ   վառեցն երկինք եւ
    երկիր, այսինքն   երկիր որպէս
    օդ: օդ:

XIV Չորեքտասաներորդ օրն XV Հնգետասաներորդ օրն
     եղիցի երկինք եւ   եղիցի երկին եւ
     երկիր նոր.   երկիր նոր:
     եւ յարիցեն ամենայն   Յայնժամ Գաբրիէլ հրեշ-
     մեռեալք: տակապետն հրամանաւ
                             Աստուծոյ գոչէ գձայն

փողոյն ի վերայ Վիրապի մեր Լուսաւորչին, թէ աւա

Քրիստոս գա, արիք ընդ առաջ նորա. յայնժամ յառնեն

սուրբքն:

XV   On the <u>fifteenth</u> day   XIV   On the <u>fourteenth</u> day
     the heavens and the   the heavens and earth
     earth shall be burnt,   shall be burnt <u>like</u>
     <u>that</u> <u>is</u> <u>to</u> <u>say</u> the   atmosphere.
     atmosphere.

XIV On the <u>fourteenth</u> day   XV   On the <u>fifteenth</u> day
     there will be a new   there will be a new
     heaven and earth,   heaven and earth.
     and all the dead shall   Then Gabriel, the
     rise.   archangel, by God's
                                     command sounds the
                                     blast of the trumpet
over the Pit of our Illuminator, 'Behold, Christ
is coming, rise up before him.' Then the saints
arise.

De XV Signis

B	C
De Quindecim Signis	De Signis Quindecim die-rum ante judicium
Quindecim signa quinde-cim dierum ante diem judicii, invenit Hiero-nymus in annalibus Hebraeorum.	Hieronymus autem in anna-libus Hebraeorum invenit signa quindecim dierum ante diem judicii, sed utrum continui futuri sint dies illi, an inter-polatim, non expressit.
I. Prima die eriget se mare in altum quadraginta cu-bitis, super altitudines montium, et erit quasi murus, et amnes simili-ter.	Prima die eriget se mare quadraginta cubitis super altitudinem montium stans in loco suo quasi murus.
II Secunda die descendent usque ad ima, ita ut summitas eorum vix conspici possit.	Secunda tantum descendet, ut vix posset videri.
III Tertia die erunt in aequa-litate, sicut ab exordio.	Tertia marinae belluae apparentes super mare,

		dabent rugitus usque ad coelum;
IV	Quarta die pisces et omnae belluae marinae, et congregabuntur super aquas, et dabunt voces et gemitus, quarum significationem nemo scit nisi Deus.	quarta ardebit mare, et aquae;
V	Quinta die ardebunt ipsae aquae ab ortu suo usque ad occasum.	quinta herbae et arbores dabunt rorem sanguinem;
VI	Sexta die omnes herbae, et arbores sanguineum rorem dabunt.	Sexta ruent aedificia;
VII	Septima die omnia aedifica destruentur.	septima petrae ad invicem collidentur;
VIII	Octava die debellabunt petrae ad invicem, et unaquaeque in tres partes se dividet, et unaquaeque pars collidet adversus alteram.	octava fiet generalis terrae motus;

IX   Nona die erit terrae   nona aequabitur terra;
     motus qualis non fuit
     ab initio mundi.

X   Decima die omnes colles   decima exibunt homines de
     et valles in platitudinem   cavernis, et ibunt velut
     convertentur, et erit   amentes, nec potuerunt
     aequalitas terrae.   mutuo loqui.

XI   Undecima die homines   undecima surgent ossa
     exibunt de cavernis   mortuorum, et stabunt
     suis, et current quasi   super sepulcra;
     amentes, nec poterit
     alter respondere alteri.

XII Duodecima die cadent   duodecima cadent
     stellae et signa de   stellae;
     coelo.

XIII Decima tertia de congre-   tredecima morientur
     gabuntur ossa defuncto-   viventes, ut cum mortuis
     rum, et exsurgent usque   resurgent;
     ad sepulcrum.

XIV Decima quarta die omnes   quartadecima ardebit
     homines morientur, ut   caelum, et terra;
     simul resurgant cum
     mortuis.

XV. Decima quinta die ardebit   quintadecima fiet

    terra usque ad inferni   coelum novum, et terra

    novissima, et post erit   nova, et resurgent

    dies iudicii.   omnes.

C continues:

Et addidit Jesus: "Sicut fulgur exit ab oriente et
paret usque in occidentem, sic erit adventus Filii
hominis (Matt 24:27, cf. Luke 27:24)," subitus scilicet,
et coruscus, et tunc apparebit signum Filii hominis in
coelo, id est in aere, supra locum unde ascendit, et
ante eum erunt instrumenta mortis suae, quasi vexilla
triumphi, crux, clavi, lancea, et in carne ejus vide-
buntur cicatrices, ut videant in quem pupugerunt
(Rev 1:7), et in valle Josephat judicabitur omnis homo,
angelis congregantibus eos (Mark 12:27).
*Additio 1. Nota quod dicitur judicium futurum in vale
  Josephat. Sed nota quod tunc non erit vallis, quia
  quarto decimo die aequabitur terra, sed contra illum
  locum erit. Vel propter interpretationen hujus nominis
  Josephat, interpretatur enim judicium. Vallis ergo
  Josephat, humilitatem judicii sonat.

COMMENTARY ON THE ARMENIAN TEXT

Superscription: I clearly lacks all of the Christian
elements which may be discerned in II. The last sentence in II, "There are fifteen signs before the coming
of Christ" is exactly parallel in function to the latter
part of the sentence in I. The preceding material in II
refers to the witness of the Sacred Scripture, of Apostles, and of prophets to the destruction of the world
as described in the following. This is, in our view, an
expansion, since there is no further reference to any
scriptural verse or proof text throughout all of the
following Armenian document. In principle, it would
seem unlikely that I was derived from II, while II might
represent an "Armenization" of a text like I (See also
Introductory Remarks above).

Day I: The variation between the recensions does not
affect the meaning. The flood referred to is clearly
an eschatological repetition of Noah's flood, as is
indicated by the mention of how high the water rose
above the highest mountains (cf. Gen 7:20). The actual
measure of depth differs, the Bible giving fifteen
cubits, as against our text's forty (see on Hebrew version). The very destruction by flood is strange, in
view of God's covenant with Noah (Gen 9:11, cf. 8:21,22).
Few parallels to this idea can be found in the chief
listings of similar events. The phrase "like a wall" is
reminiscent of Exod 14:22,29 etc.

Ancient parallels: Arm. 4 Ezra 6:20, Seventh
Vision of Daniel p. 42, lns. 15-6.

Day II: The variation between the two Armenian recensions, although substantial from a textual viewpoint,
makes no major difference in meaning.

Ancient parallels: T. Levi 4:1, 4 Ez 6:24, Ap.Elij.
3:63, Ps.-Hippolytus, De consum. mundi 27 (P.G.10.929-932):
cf. As. Moṣ. 10:6.[24]

Day III: Recension II adds to the contents of I the
idea of the death and putridity of the fish and whales.
In its text for this day, for the first time, two of
those late, post-classical grammatical forms are encountered, which are typical of this text, viz. մեռանեն
and հուրեցնեն.

Ancient parallels: Jub. 23:18, Lactantius, Instit.
VII,16,8; exactly parallel - Ephraem Syrus texts apud
Bousset, Antichrist, pp. 195 ff. Ps. - Hippolytus,
De consum mundi 27 (P.G. 10.929).

Day IV: Here once more, recension II introduces features additional to those found in recension I.   "The
trees" are added to the list of flora (cf. Latin B C)
which, as well as dripping blood, also dry and wither.

Ancient parallels: 4 Ezra 5:5, Barn. 12:1, Ladder
of Jacob 7; cf. Sib. Or. 3:684, 804.

Day V: Here the text preserved by the two recensions of
Armenian is identical, except for a minor variation of
verb form.

It is noteworthy that there is a certain irration-
ality running through all of these signs as they are
presented in the text. The very first event adnumbrated,
the flood, is described as being so severe as to reach
a depth of forty cubits and destroy the whole earth. Yet,
plants still exist until Day IV, buildings are only
overthrown on Day V, while the intervening events make

---

24. The ultimate background may lie in the myth that
has also informed passages such as Isa 51:10 and others
in the Bible. On this see, in general: F.M.Cross Jr.,
"The Divine Warrior in Israel's Early Cult", Biblical
Motifs: Origins and Transformations, ed. A. Altmann,
Cambridge, Mass. Harvard, (1966) 11-30.

the survival of the troglodytes of Day X, or of the "all
men" of Day XIII rather unlikely, to say the least.   On
the other hand, occasional groups of two or three days
seem to be held together by a logical or at least a
plausibly coherent structure.   Such are Days I, II and
III, which move from flood, through drying up of the
sea, to the death of maritime creatures and see further
observations on these, below.   The same seems to be
true of Days VIII and IX and Days XIV and XV.   There is,
however, no embracing concept, such as a movement from
a lesser to a more general measure of destruction, which
controls the overall ordering of the signs.   Furthermore, either Day VII or Day XIV seems to be redundant,
and other equally anomalous features may be observed.

Ancient Parallels: Apocalypse of Thomas, 556-7.

Day VI: Again, recension II adds certain elements
absent from I, notably the thundering of the rocks and
their destruction.   The verb $\rho\iota h^{\gamma}$ "destroyed" is
written with a ρ "b" instead of the correct ψ
"p".   This makes it likely that the scribe responsible
for this error spoke a dialect in which ρ "b" was
pronounced as "p", as in Modern West Armenian.

Ancient Parallels: Sib.Or.3:680-681, T. Levi 4:1,4
Ezra 4:5, Ap. Elijah 3:84, cf. Ezek 38:20, I Enoch 50:
6-7, As. Mos. 10:4.

Day VII: According to Latin, only the sea burns at this
point, while all versions have a general conflagration
on Day XIV, q.v. In Armenian, however, a more cosmic
dimension is implied, and so some general parallels may
be included at this point.   The idea of a burning of the
world with fire is rather widespread in eschatological
writings.

Ancient Parallels: fire originates from earth 4
Ezra 5:8; from heavens Sib.Or. 2:196-197, 3:542-543,
690, 2 Apoc. Bar. 27:10. Geniza Daniel Apocalypse, ln.36,

Seventh <u>Vision</u> <u>of</u> <u>Daniel</u>, p. 42 lns. 16-7, <u>The</u> <u>Last</u>
<u>Vision</u> <u>of</u> <u>Daniel</u>, p. 47; from heaven and earth <u>Ap. Elijah</u>
3:82; general conflagration Josephus <u>Ant</u>. I, 70; Philo,
<u>Vit</u>. <u>Mos</u>. 2:263; <u>Vit</u>. <u>Ad</u>. 49-50; cf. <u>Agadat</u> <u>Bereshit</u>
(Jellinek, <u>B.M.</u> 4)1; <u>2 Apoc. Bar.</u> 70:8 .[25]

<u>Day</u> <u>VIII</u>: The same underlying dialectical feature, ob-
served in a note on Day VI above, also appears here. The
form ընթ՛շանուր of II reads թ "t" for դ "d" which latter was probably pronounced by the scribe as "t".

    Ancient parallels: Ezek 38:14, 4 Ezra 6:20, <u>Sib</u>.
<u>Or</u>. 3:675, <u>2 A.Bar</u> 70:8, Matt 24:7, <u>Sefer Eliyahu</u> ln.23
Geniza Daniel Apocalypse, ln. 41 <u>et</u> <u>al</u>.

<u>Day</u> <u>IX</u>: The verb form of II, apparently an active for a
medio-passive, recurs below and is doubtless dialectal.
The levelling of the mountains is probably to be regard-
ed as the outcome of the earthquake.

    Ancient parallels: <u>Sib</u>. <u>Or</u>. 8:236, Lacantius, <u>In-</u>
<u>stitut</u>. VII, 16, 11; cf. Isa 40:4 (context differs). [26]

<u>Day</u> <u>X</u>: The idea of men hiding from the fear of God in
caverns and caves is to be found in Isa 2:10, and particularly 19 and 21. It is there used in a context of a

25. This is probably not the "testing" fire referred to
by T. Abr. A,13, Didache 14:5. For a selection of later
sources see: Bousset, <u>Antichrist</u> 238-245. The idea of
the cataclysmic fire is well known in Greek thought. See
e.g., the material cited by J. Burnet, <u>Early</u> <u>Greek</u> <u>Phil-</u>
<u>osophy</u> (rep; London: Black, 1945)157-160. The sources
are manifold. See also: T.F. Glasson, <u>Greek</u> <u>Influence</u>
<u>in</u> <u>Jewish</u> <u>Eschatology</u>, (London: 1961) 77-80, who
guotes some further details. On this concept in Jewish
sources, see the detailed treatment by L.Ginzberg, "Mab-
bul Shel Esh", <u>Hagoren</u> 8 (5672), 35-51 [in Hebrew].
26. It may be observed that passages relating signs and
portents accompanying theophanies have much in common
with the Messianic signs. <u>Sib</u>. <u>Or</u>.3:683-692, describing
God's warlike theophany has, inter alia, the falling of
walls, flooding by torrents of blood, rocks flowing with
blood, fire, and cataclysms of rain. The investigation
of this subject, however, would be tangential to the aim
of the present study.

prophecy of God's epiphany to exact judgement from the
wicked. The verses in Isaiah combined to produce a clear
picture of men hiding themselves in caverns and clefts
of rocks in order to escape God's judgement. They were
taken up also by Rev 6:15-16, at the opening of the
sixth seal. There seems to be no reason to regard The
Signs as derived from Revelation rather than from Isaiah.
Indeed, there appear to be some indications that the
contrary is the case. Where The Signs is almost literally identical with Isaiah 2:19, "caves...and rocks of
the mountains". The Latin version reads in cavernis,
which is not helpful in making the determination. This
feature is also found in Seventh Vision of Daniel, p.41,
lns. 26-7. The Armenian terms differ from The Signs.
Less similar is Mark 13:14. The balance of the descrip-
tion in The Signs has no parallel elsewhere.[27]

27. It might be maintained that the stars are said to
fall both in Revelation and in The Signs and that this
indicates that The Signs is dependent on Revelation.
Yet, in this latter work, the falling of the stars precedes the incident of the caves and is an integral part
of a list of astronomical portents, none of the others
of which is found in The Signs (except for the commonplace earthquake). In The Signs the falling of the
stars follows the caves and is separated by the distinctive falling of the dead from their tombs. In Latin
B this is not the case, but its order of events is secondary. The falling of the stars is very common in the
lists of the Messianic woes (see below). It seems,
therefore, that no significance should be attached to
the conjunction of these elements. Incidentally, the
falling of the stars also takes its origin in the Book
of Isaiah (34:4). Compare also Otot Hamashiah (Jellinek,
B.M. 3) 50. The caves and caverns occur in a number of
texts as the places to which the righteous flee when the
Antichrist comes. For a selection see: Bousset, 212
ff., cf. Ps. Hippol. De consum mundi 32 (P.G. 10 p.936)
In these texts, on the whole, there is no clear evidence
of dependence on Revelation and it is likely that some
common tradition is here involved, as Bousset, indeed,
suggests.

<u>Day XI</u>: There is no really significant difference be-
tween the two recensions. In I, the dead go from their
tombs, while in II, they fall from them. This is a mac-
abre portent and not the issuing forth of the dead for
resurrection. In the Latin versions, the bones of the
dead are gathered together and they rise up in their
tombs. No parallels are known, unless it be the saints
rising from their tombs at the crucifixion, Matt 27:52.
See also Commentary on Hebrew version.

<u>Day XII</u>: There are certain anomalous features in the
language of this sentence. The verb is active in II
instead of the medio-passive of I (see note on Day IX,
above). The variation between the recensions does not
affect the import of the passage.

Ancient parallels: Matt 24:29, <u>Seventh</u> <u>Vision</u>
<u>of</u> <u>Daniel</u> p. 42, lns. 14-5, Rev 6:13 - all dependent on
Isa 34:4; <u>Sib</u>. <u>Or</u>. 2:202, Lactantius, <u>Institut</u>. VII.16,
8-10, <u>Book of John the Evangelist</u> p. 192, Ps. Hippolytus,
<u>de consum. mundi</u> 37 (<u>P.G.</u> 10:940).

<u>Day XIII</u>: The variant verb form of recension II is iden-
tical with that noted above, see notes on Day IX.

<u>Day XIV</u>: In I, fairly obviously, the numbering of the
fourteenth and fifteenth days has been reversed. Recension II, at this point, has preserved the original order.
The idea of the conflagration was discussed above (see
note on Day VII). The burning described in the present
context is apparently of more universal measure than that
of Day VII. The final phrase is unclear in Armenian and
is missing from Latin.

Ancient parallel: Ps. -Hippolytus, <u>De consum</u>.
<u>mundi</u> 37 (<u>P.G.</u> 10.940).

Day XV: The idea of the new heavens and the new earth is very widespread, and there is no point in documenting it here.

Conclusion: The form of the Conclusion in recension II clearly indicates its Armenian origin. The final phrase of I could be Jewish or Christian, Greek, Latin or Armenian. The blowing of the trumpet here is unlike 4 Ezra 6:23 where it has a different function and meaning, but may be compared with Didache 16:6, Seventh Vision of Daniel, p. 47, Otot Hamashiah (Jellinek, B.M.2)61-2 , Lactantius, Institut. VII, 16, 11, and many other sources.

HEBREW VERSION

א 257   חמש עשרה אותות לפני יום הדין

מספר ירחמיאל:

והמים גברו חמש עשרה אמה ממעל

להרים בימי המבול כי כן נתמלאה

כל מחטאת בני האדם וכן יעשה

ליום הדין כאשר נעשה

במבול, כי ביום הדין ישפט הק‹דוש›

את עולמו באש שנ' כי באש

5   יייי נשפט:/ ויגדל האש

עד חמש עשרה אמה ממעל להר תבור מכל

ההרים הוא הר הנקרא

אולימפוס, כי מאותו הר עשו היונים

את מניין האולימפיאדס, כי לארבעה שנים

היו עולים בהר אולימפוס והיו כותבין

בעפר תיחו‹ח› אשר על

ההר את נצחונם, ולא היה רוח מנשב עליו

מפני גובהו כי האו‹יר› לא היה

10   ‹שולט› עליו וגם עוף השמים/לא

פורח עליו ואיש לא היה עולה עליו

אם לא היה נותן בעין ספוג מלא מים

ונחיריו מפני האויר.

ולפני יום הדין חמשה עשר יום

יהיו מופתים בשמים ובארץ,

257r   Fifteen Signs before the Day of Judgement

from The Book of Jerahmeel

And the waters increased to fifteen cubits above

the mountains in the days of the Flood for thus every-

thing was filled with the sins of men and thus will it

happen on the day of judgement as happened in the

Flood.   For on the day of judgement the Ho⟨ly⟩ One will

judge his world as it says, "For by fire will the Lord

5 execute judgement" (Isa 66:16)./ And the fire will in-

crease to fiteen cubits above Mt. Tabor, (and above

the highest) of all mountains, the mountain called

Olympus.   For, from that mountain the Greeks made the

reckoning of the Olympiads.   For, each four years they

would ascend Mount Olympus and they would write their

victories in the dust of the soft ear⟨th⟩ which was on

the mountain.   And the wind did not blow upon it be-

cause of its height for the atm⟨osphere⟩ had no

10 ⟨control⟩ over it.   The birds of the heavens too / do

not flutter over it and people did not ascend it un-

less they placed a sponge soaked with water in their

eye(s) and in their nostrils because of the air.

Fifteen days before the day of judgement there

will be portents in the heavens and on the earth, and

והיתה צרה גדולה אשר לא נהייתה

מהיות גוי על הארץ.

ותרעש הארץ ונמסו ההרים

ושאון ימים יהמיון לפלגים

אשר ישח האדם בפחד לבו

15   כי קרוב יום י״י/על כל

הגוים   הוא יום י״י לא יכילו זעמו

ולא יושע כל בשר

כי אם בתשובת   עזיבת

רשעו וישוב אל י״י.

ואלה האותות חמש עשרה בחמשה עשר יום

כל אחד ואחד ביומו:

I   ביום הראשון יצא הים

מחוק גבולו על כל גדותיו

20   וירבו המים /ממעל להרים הגבוהים ארבעים אמה

ויעמדו כחומה.

II   ביום השיני ישובו ויחרבו

עד למעט.

III   ביום השלישי יתראו התנינים הגדולים

אשר בתוך הים מחוסר המים

והם בַּלַיְיִנֶשׁ והם גועים

בקולם עד לשמים.

IV   ביום הרביעי יבשו ויחרבו כל המים שבימים

there will be great distress such as has not been from

the time of existence of nations upon the earth. And

the earth will quake and the mountains will melt and

the tumult of the seas will roar in (its) streams,

which a man shall relate to his son in fear of his

15 heart that the day / of the Lord is close upon all the

nations, that is the day of the Lord which his anger

will not contain and all flesh will not be saved ex-

cept by repentance of (i.e. which is) abandoning its

evil; and he will return to the Lord.

And these are the fifteen signs on fifteen days,

each individual one on its day.

I   On the first day the sea will issue forth from the

limit of its boundary over all its shores and the wat-

20 er will rise to forty cubits / above the high mount-

ains and will stand like a wall.

II   On the second day it will subside and dry up until

(it is) few.

III   On the third day the great sea-monsters which are

in the sea will be visible because of the lack of wat-

ter, and they are the balaenas, and they low with

their voice to the heavens.

IV   On the fourth day all the waters in the seas and

ובאגמים ובנהרות ויצמא

25   ויהמה האדם / והבהמה והעוף:

V   ביום החמשי יבכו האדם והבהמה והעוף

למים עד שיטיפו דם מעיניהם

וכל האילנות והדשאים יטיפו דם:

VI   ביום הששי יהיו קולות וברקים

ורעמים ורוחות:

VII ביום השביעי יכתתו כל האבנים

וימסו:

VIII ביום השמיני תרעש ותגעש הארץ

ומוסדות השמים ירגזון:

30   IX   ביום התשיעי יפלו / הבתים

ויפלו המדרגות ויצעקו העצים

והאבנים כצעקת בני אדם:

X   ביום העשירי יכנסו ויבאו בני האדם בסעיפי

הסלעים ובמחילות עפר

מפני פחד יייי:

XI   ביום אחד עשר ינערו עצמות בני אדם

מקבריהם ויושלכו ויסחבו

על פני חוצות:

XII ביום שנים עשר יפלו הכוכבים והמאורות

ונגולו השמים (כ) ספר

35   והארץ / כבגד תבלה

lakes and rivers will become dry and dry up and man,

25 beast, and bird will thirst / and groan.

V   On the fifth day man, beast, and bird will weep

for water until they drip blood from their eyes and

all the trees and the grasses will drip blood.

VI   On the sixth day there will be sounds and light-

ning and thunder and winds.

VII   On the seventh day all the stones will be smashed

and melt.

VIII On the eighth day the earth will rock and reel and

the foundations of the heavens will tremble.

I   30IX   On the ninth day / the houses will fall and the

terraces (or: cliffs) will fall and the trees and

stones will cry out as a human cry.

X   On the tenth day men will enter into the clefts

of the cliffs and holes of the ground because of the

terror of the Lord.

XI   On the eleventh day the bones of men will be

aroused from their graves and will be cast and dragged

through the streets.

XII   On the twelfth day the stars and the luminaries

will fall and the heavens will be rolled up as a book

35 and the earth will wear out / like a garment and the

ויפתחו הקברות ויתקעו

השופרות ורבים יקיצו:

XIII ביום שלשה עשר ימותו

ויגוע כל בשר יחד:

XIV 2571 בר ביום ארבעה/עשר ישרפו שמים וארץ

וימסו מאש הגדולה

ויכלו:

XV   ביום חמשה עש ר יבראון בגה שמים החדשים

והארץ החדשה ויקיצו

שוכני עפר המשכילים ויזהירו

כזוהר הרקיע

וכצאת השמש בגבורתו

ויקבצו בתוך ירושלים עיר הקודש

ויראו עין בעין

בשוב ה' ציון

5   ויאספו / אל עמק יהושפט

לשפט אותם ואז יבראון כולם

ברוח חדשה ונפש חדשה וברייה חדשה

ויבאו לפני המלך ה':

Vacat 12 let and then continues with Ps. Philo, Bib. Ant. 10:3ff.

4 הק>דוש<   הק̇ <   6-7 אולימפוס...אולימפיאדס... אולימפוס[

קו מאוזן מעל ל-סמ״ר | 8 תיחו>ח < תיחוה | 9

<שולט[שלולט למי״ד ו°מחוקה בקו | 10 האו>יר<   האו |

29 >נגולו[<   נגואלו | >כ <ספר] הספר |

38 >ה < שמים[שמים

graves will be opened and the trumpets will be

blown and many will awake.

XIII   On the thirteenth day they will die and all

flesh will perish together.

257v XIV   On the four/teenth day heaven and earth will

be burnt and melt in the great fire and be des-

troyed.

XV   On the fifteenth day < the > new heavens and

the new earth will be created * and those wise who

dwell in the dust shall awake and will shine like

the brightness of the firmament (Dan 12:2-3) * and

like the sun as it rises in its might (Jud 5:31).

And they shall be gathered in the midst of the holy

city Jerusalem * and eye to eye they will see the

return of the Lord to Zion (Isa 52:8).   And they

5 will be gathered / to the valley of Jehosaphat for

their judgement and then they will all be created

with a new spirit and a new soul and a new crea-

tion and they will come before the king, the Lord.

(Continues L.A.B. 10:3ff.)

COMMENTARY ON THE HEBREW VERSION

Title (line 1): The title clearly indicates the origin
of the fragment in the Book or Chronicles of Jeraḥmeel.
The rest is obvious and is also similar to the titles of
Latin and Armenian.

Introduction (lines 2-11).

The first point made by the introduction is the typ-
ological relationship between Noah's Flood and the flood
which is expected at the eschaton. Just as Noah's Flood
covered the highest mountains, so will the flood of fire.
This relationship was made explicit also in the descrip-
tion of the flood of water which will take place on Day I
according to the Armenian version. The problems inherent
in it were pointed out in the commentary to that place.
In the Introduction to the Hebrew version here, the measure of fifteen cubits is drawn from Gen 7:20 and is not
brought into agreement with that of forty cubits in the
text of Day I. This fact probably indicates that the introduction of Noah's flood into this context is secondary. 28

The sentence tying Mount Tabor to Mount Olympus
seems to be incomplete. This prevents the precise ascer-
taining of the way in which the legend about Mount Olympus was related to the line of thought of this paragraph.
The height of Mount Tabor was apparently the point d'ap-
pui for the introduction of a short passage dealing with

---

28. The origins of the flood of fire are discussed in
the commentary to Day VII, supra. The continuation of
the text in the manuscript deals with the resolution of
a possible conflict between the covenant with Noah and
the future flood of fire. Inter alia it predicts that
for forty years before the day of judgement there will
be no rainbows because of the aridity which will prevail
at that time.

some traditions associated with Mount Olympus, traditions
designed to illustrate its great height. Its lofty elevation was a subject of traditional lore as is clear from
Isidore of Seville's writings and other sources quoted
above. In them the idea is found that the mountain is so
high that the winds do not reach its peak. This forms
the first part of the tradition found in the Hebrew version of The Signs. The second part of the legend in The
Signs is without parallel known to this writer. Nonetheless, there seems no reason to doubt that it origina-
ted in some mediaeval embroidery on the legendary geogra-
phy of Greece. The absence of the birds and the need to
block the eyes and nostrils may have a relationship to
the thin atmosphere encountered at great heights.

Two textual comments may be made on this section. In
line 2, the reading נתמלאה כל is completely clear in the
manuscript. It is grammatically anomalous, however, and
perhaps is a case of wrong division for נתמלא הכל .
Second, the reading הָאֲנ<י>ר > "the air" is somewhat con-
jectural; the first three letters alone are found in the
manuscript. Like אויר in line 12, the word here means
"the atmosphere" or perhaps even "the weather", showing
a semantic range like Greek ἀήρ, Latin aer.

Introduction (lines 11-16)

The second paragraph of the introduction is a sort
of summary of the text which follows. It introduces the
idea that the coming evils can be avoided by repentance,
an idea which finds no echo in any of the other texts and
seems to be out of place in view of the ideas of the document as outlined above.

In lines 14-15 the words translated "relate to his
son in fear that the day ..." could also be rendered
"relate to his son in fear. For the day ...".

In the text, the phrase אשר לא יכילו זעמו "which his
anger will not contain" is somewhat rough as it stands.

One might suppose that this goes back to a reading like
לא יכלה זעמו   "his anger will not cease" (line 15).

Day I (lines 19-20): The actual text for the first day is
preceded by a second title which may be original to the
text, with the title to the introduction (line 1) having
been added together with the introduction.

The words "from the limit --- shores" should be compared with Jer 5:22. The expression rendered "rise to"
could be translated literally "increase to".

Day II (lines 20-21): This sign is identical in content
in the other versions. The word ישוכן "subsided" is that
used of the waters of the Flood in Gen 8:1. Corresponding to "until (they were) few", the other versions read
"to a depth" or "the depths" and also add an additional
clause.

Day III (lines 21-23): The mediaeval Hebrew form יתראו
corresponds to Latin apparentes. Hebrew reads merely "sea-
monsters", like the "whales" of B and I, not "fish and
whales", like C and II. The sea-monsters appear on the
face of the sea as in the Latin version, not on the face
of the "waters" like in the Armenian. The words מחוסר מים
"because of the lack of water" are not paralleled in
the other versions. The word balaenas is added to explain what the תנינים were. This should be contrasted
with the belluae marinae of B and C.

Day IV (lines 23-25): This sign, the drying up of the
sea, is apparently equivalent to the burning of the sea
which is attested by all other versions. This shows the
structural similarity of the Hebrew version to the Latin
for in B and C texts this sign follows that of the
whales. In both Armenian texts the order is different
and this sign comes on Day VI.

Despite this, the text and content of this sign are

very different from those of the Latin and Armenian versions. It is probable that the text of Hebrew is secondary here, for the drying up of the sea is already implied by the sign of the second day in Latin and Armenian
and is stated actually to have taken place on that day by
the Hebrew version itself. This is why the whales are
stranded in the sign of Day III, and see in detail the
Commentary to these days above. The motive for the
transformation which the text has undergone in the Hebrew
version is not evident.

Day V (lines 25-27): The words "man and beast --- eyes"
have no obvious parallels. It should be noted that once
again Hebrew agrees with the Latin B and C which read
herbae et arbores,rather than with Armenian "trees".
This, together with the cases pointed out in the commentary here on other days, is a clear indication of the
relationship of the Vorlage of Hebrew with the type of
text preserved in Latin.

Day VI (line 25): This sign has no parallel in content in
Armenian and Latin B and C. In them, following the trees'
dripping blood is the portent of the destruction of buildings. In the Hebrew version this portent has been combined with the levelling of the mountains which occurs as
sign IX here and in the corresponding position in the
other versions. This perhaps is a result of the attempt
to organize the material more systematically, placing the
destruction of the buildings and the levelling of the
mountains after the great earthquake. It may also have
been facilitated by Ezek 38:20, see Day IX, below. The
word קולות could also be rendered "thunder", but this
translation has been used for the unambiguous רעמים
later in the sentence.

Day VII (line 28): The other versions do not have the
words "and melt". They might be compared to the "and be

destroyed" of Armenian II, but these seem more likely to
be parallel, conjunctive developments rather than to reflect a common original.

Day VIII (lines 28-29): The text for this day is typical
of the biblicizing character of the Hebrew version. Latin and Armenian have a prediction of an earthquake at
this point. In Hebrew the verse 2 Sam 22:8 is quoted
verbatim, with a reversal of the first two verbs. This
caused the introduction of the shaking of the foundations of the heaven, a feature is drawn from that verse.
The archaizing ending   וו- of the final verb
     should be noted. It does not occur in the Massore-
tic text, but it is also found on the verb   יבראון
in the conclusion of The Signs and so is probably typical of the translator.

Day IX (lines 29-31): The composite nature of this material was noted in the observations on Day VI, supra.
It might be suggested, in addition to the possibilities
raised there, that the two Days were drawn together by
the identity of the verb with which they both open,
יפלו . In any case, the combination of the two texts is
clear here. The other versions have the levelling of
the mountains as the chief characteristic of this verse.
Again, its love of biblical quotation comes to the fore
when the Hebrew version draws its phrase for this from
Ezek 38:20. This obscures somewhat the point of the
portent which Latin formulates as aequabitur terra (C).
On the origins of this expectation, see Commentary to
Armenian, Day IX, above.
     In 4 Ezra 5:5 the stones are said to give voice, but
no clear parallels to this eschatological cry of the
trees have been observed.[29]

---

29. The talking tree of T. Abr A3, B3 is of a quite dif-
ferent character, as are the parallels adduced by M. R.
James, The Testament of Abraham ("Texts and Studies",
II.2 ; Cambridge 1892) p. 59-64.

Day X (lines 31-32): The form of text for this day
found in Hebrew is almost a word for word quotation of
Isa 2:21 into which are incorporated two words from
Isa 2:19. The eschatological application of these verses became widespread, see the observations in the Commentary to Armenian, Day X, above. The text as presented in the Hebrew version, then, shows none of these
peculiar characteristics which distinguish the use of
this material in the Latin and Armenian traditions from
its uses in early Christian sources. In the Latin and
Armenian versions the portent is not men's concealment
in the crannies or the rocks, but their issuing forth
from them. Moreover, according to these two versions
those men who come forth from the rocks will be mad and
will run about and be unable to talk to one another.
Hebrew then provides a form of text which is both "biblicizing" and also in line with the more generally ac-
cepted understanding of the eschatological interpretation of these verses.[30]

Day XI (lines 32-33): The order of omens and days
agrees with Latin C and Armenian, not with Latin B. The
raising of the bones from the graves is couched in language drawn from Jer 22:19. The phraseology of Hebrew,
which refers to the bones, is like that of Latin, while
the Armenian version refers simply to "the dead".

Day XII (lines 33-35): In the other versions this sign
relates the falling of the stars and (according to
Latin B) of portents from the heavens. This has brought
Isa 34:4 to mind and the first part of this verse is
then quoted. The last part of the biblical verse,
however, refers to the "withering" of the heavenly host,

---

30. This interpretation does not seem to have been
current in Rabbinic sources, but it is nonetheless
ancient, see Commentary to Armenian Day X, supra.

using the word יבול . This word had two effects. The
first is that its phonetic similarity to יפולי "will
fall" used of the stars by The Signs provided an additional basis for association of Isa 34:4. At the same
time, this verbal root was the connection for the introduction of Isa 51:6. This combination of verses widens
the scope of the upheaval referred to in the other versions.

　　　　More difficult is the addition at the end of this
day. This talks first of an opening of the graves and
blowing of trumpets, and then quotes a little fragment
of Dan 12:3 apparently referring to a partial resurrection. Problematic is that all of this is followed by
the death of all men, then by the end of the world, new
creation, and resurrection of the dead; a more extensive
quotation from Dan 12:3 is used to the same end. The
various elements involved here are found in one or another place in the other versions, but not in the prophecy for this day or for this stage of the eschatological process. No explanation for the latter part of this
verse is evident, nor does it appear to conform to any
known eschatological pattern. On the role of the trumpet, see Commentary to Armenian, Day XV, above.

Day XIII (line 36): The death of all men is the common
content of this sign in the versions. Notable is a certain roughness in the Hebrew. The first verb is plural
and the second singular; a plural subject is not readily
evident. It is possible that יחד "together" is related
to a text of the type of Latin ut cum mortibus resurgent.
The actual phrase comes from Job 34:15.

Day XIV (line 36-fol. 257v line 1): The words "and melt
--- destroyed" have no parallels in the other versions.

Day XV (lines 1-6): In fact the first part of this text
is parallel to the other versions and to the beginning

of the quotation of Dan 12:2. This has been connected
to the words et resurgent omnes and then the following
verses strung onto it in such a way as to offer no convenient break at which one might nicely distinguish the
end of Day XV and the beginning of the concluding materials. In the translation, the start of the quotations
has been marked by an asterisk and their conclusion by
the verse reference in parentheses. The reference to
the valley of Jehosaphat as the place of judgement is
based on Joel 4:12 which is not quoted literally. The
last sentence is not biblical, except for the phrase
"the king, the Lord" (Ps 98:6). This section with its
catena of biblical citations bears a general resemblance
to the concluding comments in the text of Peter Comestor
with its New Testament excerpts.

PART TWO

ONOMASTICA SACRA

I

Introductory Remarks

In the Armenian tradition there was an extensive development of the Onomastica Sacra, the lists of biblical names together with their translations or "etymologies". Three Armenian lists of this were published by F. Wutz in 1914 - 1915[1]. The most extensive of these was his first list (hereinafter: Ona I). He edited this list, which contains 880 lines in the form published, on the basis of eight manuscripts. He published a second list, containing about 50 names and their explanations, on the basis of a single manuscript (Ona II), and a third, also drawn from a single manuscript contained 702 lines (Ona III). Up to the present, Wutz' is the only scholarly publication of these lists and in his book he attempts to locate them within the broader spectrum of the onomastic lists in various languages.

A second scholarly reference to these texts is by H.M. Amalyan in a book devoted to the extensive vocabularies, dictionaries, and onomastic lists found in mediaeval Armenian manuscripts. Evidently, Amalyan was not conscious of the existence of Wutz' study. In his book he lists a great many manuscripts of the Onomastica Sacra contained in the collection of the Matenadaran in Erevan, Armenia.

Wutz' study is marred by two faults. First, his published texts are based on a very limited range of manuscripts, as is evident from the list of manuscripts presented below. Second, his work is marked by very many typographical errors, chiefly in the Armenian text,

---

1. For bibliographical references, here and in the following, see the bibliographical list, pp. xiii-xvi above.

but occasionally in the notes. Moreover, the examination
of a broader range of manuscripts than he consulted
showed that there are other lists of which he was ignor-
ant. With all these reservations, however, his study
remains basic. Until there is a new, major edition of
those texts which he published, his edition is indispen-
sable. His analysis of all the onomastica in the various languages has no substitute.

A brief perusal of the appended, preliminary list
of manuscripts (Section VII, below) indicates that the
preparation of a complete and exhaustive edition of the
Armenian Onomastica Sacra would be a formidable task,
extending beyond the modest aims of the present work.
These are just to publish some new material, not included in the works of Wutz and Amalyan. These data are
drawn, primarily, from manuscripts in the library of the
Armenian Patriarchate of Jerusalem. To these manuscripts
have been added the texts contained in four codices in
the library of the Mechitarist Fathers in Venice, in one
codex from Paris not consulted by Wutz, and in one codex
from Erevan.[2] If these twenty one new manuscripts are
combined with the nine manuscripts used by Wutz, a total
of thirty manuscripts is reached.

Wutz, as observed above, published three different
lists, which have been dubbed here Ona I, Ona II, and
Ona III. New information is offered on his Ona I and
Ona III and on three unknown lists. These new lists are
the following:

Ona IV - A short list, contained in Paris, Bibliothèque
Nationale arm. 140 (no. 66). This list is a witness to
the long list (Ona I). It contains some elements additional to the long list, but these are not onomastic in

---

2. It is greatly to be regretted that only one of the
numerous copies in Erevan was available to the writer.
Any attempt to carry out a definitive study of the
lists would reouire consultation of a broader range
of the manuscripts of this rich treasury.

character. They are Armenian words, drawn from the Armenian Bible. The onomastic list upon which it was based
was particularly close to MS No. 1 of Ona I. A sample
of this list is given below, and its witness is also included in the apparatus of Ona I. (The numbers in par-
theses are those of Wutz' edition of Ona I.)

Ona V - Manuscripts nos. 55 and 81 (Venice, Mechitarist
545 and Erevan Matenadaran 2261) contain a new, previously unpublished list. This is edited in full below and a
commentary on it has been prepared, according to the following principles. The text of the list is based, chiefly, upon no. 81, and the text of no. 81 has been corrected or supplemented according to the text of no. 55 in
cases of clear corruption or omission. All variants of
nos. 55 or 81 have been recorded in full in the critical
apparatus. In cases of clear corruption of both manuscripts, the editor has corrected where he could, enclos-
ing his corrections in pointed brackets. This is again
noted in the apparatus.

The commentary has been designed to show where a
name and etymology occur in Wutz' book and independent
observations have been added only where the name did not
occur in any of Wutz' sources. It is evident that this
list is akin to Ona III and the majority of the names
and etymologies given by it occur in that list. Ona V
does contain some additional elements not found in Ona
III and these include readings in common with Ona I,
readings in common with lists in other languages quoted
by Wutz (mainly Greek or Latin) and - of very consider-
able interest - readings not known in any of the onomastic sources quoted by Wutz. In the commentary attention has
been devoted, in particular, to these latter cases.

Ona VI - Jerusalem, Armenian Patriarchate 1422 (no. 82)
contains a major compilation of biblical onomastica and
vocabulary. This compilation covers almost 300 pages of

the manuscript. Following the entries for the first
letter of the alphabet(ayb), the list for the same letter from another list has been added in the codex, with
a scribal note indicating that this was something of an
after-thought. This second list is drawn from an onomasticon. No similar separate supplement occurs for any
other letter. In addition, the first list for ayb and
ben contains a number of names, interspersed in rapidly
increasing proportions with Armenian words and their
dictionary meanings.

The list appended to ayb is, in fact, another copy
of Wutz' Ona III, to which certain expansions have been
added on the base of Ona I, and sample of it has been
given below. The onomastic elements inserted into the
biblical vocabulary in no. 82 proper are of a different
character and two samples have been given, with translation and comments, under the title Ona VI. A few onomastic elements are to be found in the biblical vocabulary contained in Jerusalem, Armenian Patriarchate 1138
(1668 C.E.), pp. 283 f., but the list is primarily of
Armenian words.

The Texts

The materials here published are then, in summary
and in order of presentation:

Ona I - Four sample texts have been prepared based
on Wutz' manuscripts and the following codices in our
list: nos. 53, 54, 56, 57, 58, 59, 60, 61, 62, 63, 64,
65, 66, 78, 80, 83, 84. Observe that no. 64 contains
the full text of Ona I expanded by elements of Armenian
biblical vocabulary and of Ona VI (see below). These
samples are:

i   The Preface, which precedes the list in all the
manuscripts of it which were examined except   nos. 1, 7,
8, 57, 61, 64, 65.

ii   A list of the letters of the Hebrew alphabet and
their explanation, which follows the Onomasticon
in manuscript no. 1, follows the preface in most
other copies examined, and is omitted by manuscripts
nos. 7, 8, 55, 57, 64; no. 61 omits the names and
gives only the explanations. The photograph of no.
65 only includes the letters after k'ap'. To these
witnesses, the text of no. 14, printed by Amalyan
(p. 146) has been joined.

iii   The title of the list.

iv   A sample of the first forty names in Wutz' list. The
text is that of Wutz. The above listed manuscripts
were compared with this text, and their variants
included in the critical apparatus. Moreover, Wutz'
collations of nos. 5 and 7 were checked against the
photographs as a control sample and his collations
were found to be accurate, although marred by prin-
ter's errors of which the chief are:

ln 7 apparatus * Անշմանg*   for *Անչմանg*,
ln 30 apparatus *չարշարվմ*   for *չարշարիմ*,
ln 32 apparatus *Արկրաբվն*   for *Արկրաբիմ*,
ln 33 apparatus *պատասբանի* for *պատասխանի*.

Such errors have been corrected without further com-
ment and all other variants in Wutz' critical apparatus have been reproduced here. Manuscript no. 66
(Ona IV) does not include lns. 5, 6, 8, 9, 10, 12,
13, 14, 18, 20, 21, 22, 23, 24, 26, 27, 30, 31, 32,
34, 35, 37, 38, 39. The photographs of no. 64, were
unfortunately, incomplete and the following lns
were missing: 5, 9, 13, 14, 22, 23, 26, 27, 34, 35,
38, 40. A similar situation in manuscript 62 led
to the omission of lns 13, 15, 23, 24. None of
these omissions are noted in the apparatus.

v.   In addition to the sample texts, tables have been
prepared which enable a comparison of the order of names
in the manuscripts. As will be evident from the tables,
there are a number of different ways in which the names
were arranged in the list of this type and these may provide one of the keys for grouping its textual families.
These tables contain the first fifty names in the list,
and, after the first column in which the names are transliterated and assigned numbers, the numbers alone are
given. Only major variants in the form of the names are
noted. An unnumbered blank space indicates an omission.

     Ona III - A sample of text, forty names in scope,
is given with appropriate comparisons with Wutz' text and
Ona V in the commentary and all variants of Wutz' text in
the apparatus.

     Ona IV - As a sample of text, the full collations
of letters ayb and ben are given. The numbers in parentheses are those of the occurrence of the item in Ona I,
from which, as noted above, Ona IV has been excerpted. No
commentary is appropriate in view of the secondary character of the list. The unnumbered items are all elements
of Armenian biblical vocabulary and are added following
the onomastic material.

     Ona V - This new list is published in full with
translation and commentary. Its sources and character
have already been described.

     Ona VI - The existence Ona VI no. 82 was mentioned
above. With the readings of this manuscript are allied
certain of the readings of no. 64, particularly where
nos. 82 and 64 are opposed to Ona I. All readings common
to the two manuscripts have been compared and for Sample
i the variants of no. 64 included an apparatus. It thus
appears that no. 64 is a witness both to Ona I and to
Ona VI.

Sample i is composed of the first forty items in no. 82. The ratio of names is certainly higher than in the rest of the text, but Armenian words, Greek words, and one Hebrew word are also included. The totals are:

Onomastic elements	–	23
Armenian words	–	11
Greek words	–	4
Hebrew words	–	1
Inexplicable	–	1

The characteristics of the onomastic elements are examined in the commentary. A further group of names from the letter <u>ben</u> was also examined (Sample ii). The distribution of co-incidence of the onomastic elements found in these two samples drawn from Ona VI with the various Armenian lists is tabulated here. It should be borne in mind that sometimes one single entry of Ona VI combines different etymologies.

Agreement with:	No. of cases:	
Ona I	11	(i 1,4,6,11,14,21,25,27; ii 9,6,7,8)
Ona II	2	(i 14,21)
Ona III	6	(i 3,5,27,29,30; ii 5)
Ona V	4	(i 27; ii 3,7)
No parallels but		
explicable	6	(i 10,24,28,31,32; ii 4)
inexplicable	10	(i 2,17,21,22,38,39,40; ii 1)
expansionary	3	(i 4,25,27).

It follows that Ona VI is a list drawn from varied sources – onomastica, Greek-Armenian lexica, Armenian-Armenian lexica, and perhaps a list of Hebrew transliterations. Moreover, an analysis of its onomastic elements shows a great diversity. Not only are the chief onomastica known to us reflected, but Ona VI also contains some biblical onomastic elements not known in Wutz' sources and even some further, unidentifiable onomastic elements of unknown character.

It should further be noted that the Dictionary
edited by Eremia vardapet (1728) has incorporated a list
of words resembling Ona VI, apparently drawn from a manuscript source.

It lists all the items included in the samples offered
here, except for   i   28 (but see commentary), 31,39 and
40. It cannot be used, therefore, as an independent lex-
icographic source, but may serve as a witness to the
manuscript tradition (compare note on Ona VI ln 37,
below). It should be noted, moreover, that this dictionary also contains onomastic elements in addition to Ona
VI, including material like Ona I and Ona III. It is
worthy of closer examination by future editors of Onomastica Sacra Armenica.

List of Manuscripts: This list does not claim to be
exhaustive, but it is a rather inclusive listing of manuscripts containing onomastic lists and establishes a
series of numbers by which they are referred to throughout this study. It is suggested that this list form the
basis for future editions and studies.

Index of Names follows at the conclusion of this
section.

Transcription of the Names

All names are transcribed exactly according to the
system set forth above. It should be observed that in
Armenian ov often corresponds to Greek ω. Scribal prac-
tice is, moreover, often to add a y to final a and o.
This is a graphic convention, not reflected in traditional pronunciation. Moreover, confusion of the sounds in
each of the following series is not uncommon, d, t, t':
g, k, k'; b, p, p'. All of these phenomena remain in the
text and translation exactly as in the manuscripts
except that final, otiose y is omitted.

ONA I

SAMPLES OF TEXT

i Preface

Այս բառք բաղաձայնք. Հոմանուանց բազմածեալ, զամենայն
որ ինչ միանգամ (են) անուանք Հեբրայեցի յաւրէն եւ ի
մարգարէս. եւ ի նոր կտակարանս Թարգմանեալ եւ մեկնեալ
յեբրայեցւոյն ի յոյնս եւ ի յունէն ի Հայս կարգաւ ըստ
5 նշանագրաց ալփաբէթից երբայեցւոց թէ զինչ միաբա-
նութիւն անուանց ունիցին:

1   բարբա 54   բառ 78   + եռաՀիւսական 2 5 6 84
    + յեռաՀիւսական 53 56 59 62 78 79 83 | բաղաձայն
    84   բակձածեալ 78 83   բակձածեալք 79   բակձայնեալք
    84 | ամենայն   78 79
2   որ ինչ միանգամ}   om 53* 78   ինչ որ են 56 59 62
    ինչ որ 78 83 | յեբրայեցի 83 84 | յաւրէնս 53
    54 56 58 59 60 62 63 79 80 84
4   յեբրայեցւոգն 54 56 59 60 62 63 83   յեբրայեցոց
    84   յեբրայեցւոյ 79 | յոյնս}   յոյն 78 | յունէն
    յունագ 59 62   յունագն 60   յունագս 80 | Հայս}
    Հայ 78 79 80 83 84   + յասորի եւ ասորւոց 2

This consonant lexicon translated and interpreted all
the names which (are) in the Hebrew Law and Prophets and
in the New Testament, including homonyms, from Hebrew
into Greek and from Greek into Armenian, in order by the
letters of the alphabet of the Hebrews, whatever agreement of names (i.e. meaning) they might have.

5 *նշանագրաց} նշանագրացն 79 84 եւ զմեկնութիւն*
   նշանագրաց (նշանագրացն 83 84) 2 5 6 53^c 83 |
   լփափեից 2 ալփա 54 60 63 ալփաբեթիցն 79 80 84
   այբբեմից 83 | երրայեցոց 84 | միաբանութիւն}
   մեկնութիւն 81
6 *ունիցին անուանց 59 62 | անուանց} om 79*
   անուանցն 83 | ունին 78

ii Alphabet

1	Ալեփ.	ուսումն նշանագրաց:
	Բեթ.	բնակեա ի դմայ:
	Քամիլ.	լրումն վերագոյն {կամ ծնունդ}:
	Դաղեթ.	գրեալք բարձագոյնք:
5	Հէ.	սայ:
	Վալ.	ի սմանէ:
	Զէ.	եկեաց:
	Խեթ.	կենդանի է:
	Տեթ.	բարի է:
10	Յովդ.	սկիսբն:
	Քաբ.	դենելս:
	Դամեղ.	ուսիր:
	Մեմ.	ի սմանէ:
	Նուն.	յալիտենից:
15	Սամքաթ.	աւգնականութիւն:
	Եգ.	աղբեաւրական:
	Փէ.	բերան:
	Ծադէ.	զարդարութիւն:
	Կոփ.	կոչումն սրբութեան:
20	Րեշ.	երելելի կամ առաջնորդ:
	Շին.	ատամունք:
	Թաւ.	նշան կամ կոչումն:

1	Alep',	teaching of letters.
	Bet',	dwell in it!
	K'amil,	upper fullness or birth .
	Dałet',	higher writings.
5	Hē,	this.
	Vaw,	from this.
	Zē,	he lived.
	Xet',	he is living.
	Tet',	he is good.
10	C'ovd, (corr. for Yovd)	beginning.
	K'ab,	still.
	Łamed,	learn!
	Mem,	from this.
	Nun,	eternal.
15	Samk'at',	helpfulness.
	Ec', (corr. for Ey)	of a spring.
	P'ē,	mouth.
	Cadǝ,	ornamentation.
	Kap',	call of sanctity.
20	Reš,	visible or first.
	Šin,	teeth.
	T'aw,	sign or call.

1   om 60 | Ալիփ *2* 4 5 6 14 56 59°   Ալլիփ 3   Արիփ 53
    78   Ալիֆ 54 58 59ˣ 62 63 79 80 84   Արէֆ 83 |
    ուսուՁն } + թանագրաց կամ 53 56 59 62 | նշանագրացն
    79

2   Բէթ 3 4 14 53 54 56 58 59 60 62 78 80 83 84
    Բէդ *2* | բնակեալ 56 83   բնա 59 62 | դՁին 14
    դՁաց 54   դՁա 79 80 83

3   Գամիդ 3 4 14 53 56 58° 59 62 63 80 84   Գամիլ 54 60
    79   Գամեդ 78 83   Կամիդ 58* | լրումն վերագոյն }
    om *2* | լրումն} + լրումն 61 | վերագուն 54 58

4   Դադէթ 3 4 14 53 56 60 63 80 83   Դալէթ 59   Դալեթ 62
    Դալեդ *2* (?)   Գադէթ 54 58   Արէթ 79 Դալէթ 84   + ծնունդ
    կամ 83 | գրեալ 59 62 | բարձագոյնք}   բարձր *2-5*
    14 53 54 56 58 59 60 62 63 78 79 80 83 84 +   կամ
    ծնունդ 3 4 5 14 53* 54 56 58 59 60 62 63 78 79 80
    om 6   + կամ շալիդ շնորʻյաց 53ᶜ

5   սա 79 80

6   ի սմանէ }   րմանէ 6

7   գային 9   գի 79 | կեաց 3-6 14 53 54 56 58 59
    60 62 63 78 79 80 84   կայց *2*   կեայց 61 83

8   եթ *2* 79   Հեթ 6 Խէթ 14 53 54 56 58 59 60 62 63 |
    է }   om 78

9   Տէթ 2-6 14 53 54 56 58 59 60 62 63 78 83 | om tot
    79 84

10 Յոդ 3 4 54 56 58 60 63 80   Յոդ 6   Յոտ *2* 5 14 53 59
    62 78 83   իոդ 84 | սկիզբն 2-6 53 54 56 58-63 78-80
    83 84

11 Քափ 4 5 53 54 56 58 59 62 63 65 78 80 83   Քաափ 3
    ▌Jափ *2* | դերեւ 3

12 Դամեթ *2* 5 56 59 60 62   Դամէթ 4 58 84   Դամեզ 3 63 80
    Դամէզ 65   Լամէթ 6   Մադէթ 53ᶜ   Դամեթ 78

13 Մէմ 6 56 83 | Մեմ **t**antum post ln   22 84 |
    ի մսանէ 59

14 ուն *2*   նու 59 62   նոյն 83 | յալիտեան 2-6 14 53 54
    56 58-63 65 78 79 80 83 84

15 Մամէթ 6   Մամբամ 59 62 | ոգնակնութիւն 54 60 61 78

79 84 օգնութիւն 59 աւգնութիւն 53* 58* 65 –ական–
53° 58° յoգնութիւն 62

16   էg 2 53* 59 62 65 էյ 3 4 5 53c 54 56 58 60 63 80
      83 յ 79 էյ 84 Ային 6 | աղբերակն 2 4 5 14 54
      58 59 62 63 65 78–80 83 84 աղբիւր ակն 61 աղբերական
      3 որբերաւոր 6 | + կամ երբայր հայական 56 |+ կամ
      երբայր կայական 59 62 65

18   ազէ 2 ծազէ 53* 54 65 78 83 Սադէ 6 | գoրրութիւն
      59

19   Կoփ 6 Քուփ 84 | սրբութիւն 54* 79 | + կամ
      կոշումն հեթանոսաց սրբոց 53 56 59 62 65 | + կամ
      երեւելի 61

20   րէշ 2–6 53 54 56 58 60 78 էշ 79 80 83 84 |
      երեւելի կամ} om 61 | որ երեւել 62 | կամ} om 2–
      6 14 53 54 56 58 59 60 62 63 65 78–80 83 84

21   ին 2 | ադամունք 3

22   Թափ 1 | նշանակ 61 | նշան կամ} om 2 | կոշումն}
      կանշումն 4 5 53c 54 58 60 63* 79 84 կամ կանշումն 3

Note that Wutz' text apparently contains two misprints
in the apparatus to no. 22: կանմուլշո for կանշումն and
կամ կամշումն for կամ կանշումն . No. 79 has not entered
the initial letters, from ln. 8 to the end of the alphabet. These readings are not recorded above.

In Erevan 1500, the famous Miscellany written by Mexitar of Ayrivank, on p. 370, as an enumeration of the books of the Bible, the letters of the Hebrew alphabet are found. Since they are close, in their form, to the tradition of the onomastica, they are also given here.

Ալիփ: Բեթ: Գամեղ: Դաղեթ: Հէ: Վաւ: Զէ: Խեթ: Տեթ:

Յաւտ: Քափ: Ղամէթ: Մեմ: Նուն: Սամքաթ: Է: Փէ:

Ծագէ: Կոփ: Րեշ: Շին: Թաւ:

Alip', Bet', Gameł, Dałet', Hē, Vaw, Zē, Xet', Tet',

Yawt, K'ap', Łamēt', Mem, Nun, Samk'at', Ē, P'ē,

Cagē, Kop, Reš, Šin, T'aw.

iii Title

(1)   *Բառք եբրայեցւոց*

բառք } + ըսա 2 60   + զիրք   7 | այս բառք 6 | եբրայեց-
ոցն 78   եբրայեցւոցն 80

(2)   *Զայս բառս եբրայեցի Յանուանց ՝ճեաեւորին առաքելոց*
       Փիլունեայ թարգմանեալ էին ի լեզու յոյն:

Thus only 1. Title is omitted completely by no. 84.

(1) Words of the Hebrews

(2) These words of Hebrew names were translated into

Greek by Philo who succeeded the Apostles.

1   Ադամ.   Երկիր կոյս կամ երկիր մարմնացեալ
                            {կամ յերկրէ կամ երկիր կարմիր}:

2   Աբել.   գուլորշի սգոյ {յաստուծոյ տուեալ
                            մարգարէութիւն}:

3   Ադդա.   վայելի կամ վկայութիւն նոցա:

4   Արփաքսադ.   մարգարէութիւն տեսանել {մաքրութիւն
                            տեսանելի}:

5   Ասուր.   բերեզգոհոմն կամ միջագետք:

6   Աբրամ.   հայր մեծարոյ կամ հայր բարձրեալ կամ
                            վերամբարձ:

7   Աբրահամ.   հայր ազգաց կամ հայր ընտրեալ:

8   Ագար.   սայ պանդուխտ:

9   Աննան.   վնասեալ սրտիւ:

10   Ամարփադ.   խստութիւն չար կամ չարութիւն:

11   Աբիմելեք.   հաւր իմոյ արքայութիւն:

12   Ամմովն.   ժողովուրդ նոցա կամ որդի ազգի:

13   Ասեր.   վարձք կամ մեծութիւն կամ երանութիւն:

14   Արամ.   անէծք նոցա:

15   Ասաթ.   հաւատ:

16   Ամինադաբ.   ազգ ցանկալի:

17   Ագագ.   որթ:

18   Ամրամ.   հայր բարձրելոյ կամ ժողովուրդ
                            մեծի:

19   Ահարովն: ահա հոգի:

1	Adam,	virgin earth or incarnated earth {or from earth or red earth}.
2	Abel,	vapour of mourning {prophecy given by God }.
3	Adda,	⌜enjoyable⌝ (<u>corr. for</u> witnessing) or their witness.
4	Arp'ak'sad,	to see prophecy {visible cleanliness}
5	Asur,	⌜<u>unknown word</u>⌝ or Mesopotamia.
6	Abraam,	honoured father or elevated father or exalted.
7	Abraham,	father of nations or elect father.
8	Agar,	this sojourner.
9	Awnan,	harmed by (at) heart.
10	Amarp'aɬ	bad straitness or evil.
11	Abimeɬek',	my father's kingdom.
12	Ammovn,	their people or son of nation.
13	Aser,	reward or greatness or beatitude.
14	Aram,	their curses.
15	Asat',	faith
16	Aminadab,	desirable nation
17	Agag,	vine.
18	Amram,	father of most high or people of great one.
19	Aharovn,	behold a spirit.

20   Աբիդան.   ծառայութիւն:

21   Աքիրամ.   եղբաւր իմոյ բարձրութիւն:

22   Ասրովն.   տապանակ:

23   Առած.   պատգամ:

24   Ափփուսուվթ.   ծածուկ:

25   Անթրակ.   . . .

26   Արիովն.   իշխան կամ կատարեալ:

27   Ասերովն.   երանութիւն կամ ⌈Դաւիթ⌉ կատարեալ:

28   Ամուրհացի.   ծաղեալբ:

29   Ամադեք.   ազգ լեգուող:

30   Ադոնիբեզեկ.   տէր շարշարից:

31   Ազան.   յայնժամ այսբ:

32   Ակրաքիմ.   կարծիք:

33   Անաթովթ.   պատասխանի:

34   Արուէր.   ընդդէմ աստուծոյ:

35   Աւովդ.   խոստովանելի:

36   Աննա.   արարած նոցա:

37   Ազոտոս.   հրածին կամ . . .

38   Ասկալովն.   կշրեալ:

39   Ակկարոն.   ամլութիւն:

40   Արիմաթեմ.   լերինք:

20   Abidan,   servitude.

21   Ak'iram,   elevation of my brother.

22   Asrovn,   ark.

23   Aŕac,   command.

24   Ap'p'usovt',   secret.

25   Ant'rak,   ...

26   Ariovn,   prince or perfect.

27   Aserovn,   beatitude or perfect ⸢David⸣ (_corr._

                      for 'forecourt').

28   Amurhac'i,   having mocked.

29   Amałek',   licking nation.

30   Adonibezek,   lord of sufferings.

31   Asan,   then these.

32   Akrabim,   scorpions.

33   Anato'vt',   answer.

34   Aruēr,   against God.

35   Awovd,   confessing.

36   Anna,   their creation.

37   Azotos,   born of fire or . . .

38   Askalovn,   weighed.

39   Akkaron,   barrenness.

40   Arimat'em.   mountains.

1 երկիր կոյս} երկիր կամ երկիր կոյս 2 6 53ᶜ 61 64 78
երկիր (om 56) կամ կոյս 3 4 5 8 53* 54 56 58 62 63
65 66 83 84 | կամ երկիր- fin } om 66 | մարմնա-
ցեալ 65 մնացեալ 79 | երկիր կամ մարմնացեալ 56 |
երկիր կարմիր կամ յերկրէ (երկրէ 78) 7 53 54 56 57
59 60 62 63 65 78 79 80 83 84 | + առաւել 7

2 Աբէլ 83 84 | զլորշի սգոյ} om 2 5 6 57 61 66 78-
80 84 | յաստուծոյ- fin} om 83 | յաստուծոյ}
պաստուծոյ 54 78 յայտնեալ 53* 65 + եւ յայտնեալ 56
+ յաստուծոյ տուեալ 53ᶜ | մարգարէութիւն} + կամ
տեսանելի 3-6 8 53 54 56 58 59 60 62-65 79 80 |
+ կամ տեսուլթիւն կամ տեսանելի 84 | + կամ զլորշի
(զլորշէ 65 զորշի 56* զլորշի 56° 63 64) սգոյ
կամ զուլթ վերաբերեալ (վերաբերել 56 65) կամ երկիր
(om 64) բազմաբեր 3 4 8 53 54 56 58-60 62-65 79
80 84

3 Աղէն 2 6 57 Աղէ 78 Աղին 5 79 Ազգա 83 | վայելել
2 5 6 վկայելի 4 8 53 57 59 61 62 64 83 84 վկելի
3 վայելէ 59 79 | կամ} ի 2 5 6 57 78 79 |
վկայութեան 2 5 6 | նոցա} om 2-8 53 57 59 61 62
64 80 83 84 | + Աղին (Աղային 59 62) վկայելել
(վայել է 54 58-63) ի վկայութիւն նոցա (պստուծոյ 57
om 53 marg) 3 4 7 53 marg54 56-66 | + փափկութիւն
5

4 om totum 84 Արփաքսաթ 59 61 80 Արփագսաթ 53 marg|
տեսանելի tantum 80 | մարգարէութիւն տեսանել} om
2 57 66 | մարգութիւն 3 | տեսանել} տեսանելի
3-8 53 54 56 58-63 65 78 83 | մաքրութիւն
տեսանելի } om 3-8 53 54 56 58-63 65 78 80 |

5 բարեգոյմն 53* 59 60 62 63 բարէզոյմն 3 4 8 54
բերէզգոյումն 5 7 56 57 61 62 78 80 84 բերոյ զոյումն
53 marg բարէզոյումն 79 բերէզգամ 83 | բերէզգոյմն-
fin} om 58 | միջագետք } + կամ խորոյուրդք 3 4 7 8
53 54 56 60 63 65 79 80 + կամ (om 58) խորոյուրդք
(խորոյուրդ 84) սուրբ 5 58 84 + խորոյուրդք 59 |
միջագետ խորոյուրդս 62

6   Աբրահամ 54   57 65   Աբրաամ 61 | մեծարու 78 |

         կամ 1°-fin } om 83 | կամ-բարձրեալ}   om 2-8 53 54

         56-65 78 79 80 84 | կամ 2°}   om 59 62 | վերամ-

         բարձ } վէմ ամբարձ 59 62 | + վասն աստեղ 7

7   Աբրաամ 2-4 6 7 56 58-60 63 80 84   Աբրայամ 8 |

         ազգեաց 2 7 8 65 | հայր 2°}   om 8 | կամ հայր

         ընտրեալ }   om 6 57 61 64 66   կամ ընտրեալ հնչմանց

         2-4 7 53 54 56 58 60 63 65 78-80 83 84   կամ

         հնչմանց կամ ընտանաւորեալ 62   կամ հնչմանց կամ

         ընտպլ. 59 | + վասն իմաստասիրական բանից եւ

         գործոց 7

8   Ազարսա: պանդուխտ 56 57 | սա 78-80 84 | պան-

         տուխտ 78   պանդուխ 83

9   վնասել 83 | սրահ 65

10   Ամարփախ 7   Ամարադ 57 Ամրափադ 78 | խիստութիւն 6 |

         չար-fin}   om 84 | չար} om   2-8 53 54 56-65 78-80

         83 | + Ամարբախ խստութիւն կամ չարութիւն 8 59 62

11   Աբիմելեք 5 61   Աբիմելէք 6-8 56 58 59 62 63 66 78

         80 83   Աբիմեդեք 4 53 65   Աբիմելիք 2 54 57   Աբիմէլել

         3   Աբիմէլէք 60 79 84 | յարքայութիւն 64

12   Ամոմն 2   Ամովն 64   Ամմոն 3-5 7 53 56 59 60 62 63

         79 80 84   Ամոն 6 54 57 61 65   Ամնովն 78   Ամնոն

         83 | ժողովուրդք 62   ժողովուրանց 64 | նոցա }

         ատտուծոյ 3 om   54   illeg 58 | կամ-ազգի }   om 78

13   Ասէր 2 83 | վարձ կամ}   om 2-8 53 54 56-61 63 65

         66 78-80 83 84 | երանութիւն}   երկայնութիւն 3 4

         8 53 marg 54 56 58-60 62 63 80 84 | + կամ գովիչ

         79

14   om 79 84

15   om omn

16   Ամինադաբ 2   Ամինադամ 64* | + նա 7

17   om omn elsewhere   Ադադ (Ադազ 53*   Ազադ 61) երինչ

         (էրինչ 65) 2-8 53 54 56-65 78-80 83 | + Ազազ

         (Ազադ 65) երինչ (երինչ 7) 3 7 8 53 56 59 62 64 65 |

          + կամ երկիւղ 3 53

18   Ամրամ 1*   Արամ 54   Ամրան 79 | բարձրացելոյ 7 53 57

59-63 78-80 84 բարձրելոց 53ᶜ | ժողովուրքք 62 |
մեծի } բարձր omn

19 Աշարոն 7 56 57 63 65 Աշարան 6 | աշա } + լեառն
կամ շողի կամ բան (բերան 2 64) 2 6 57 61 64 66 |
շողի } + կամ լեառն 83   + կամ լեառն կամ (+ կամ 5)
բան (բանն 60) 4 5 7 8 53 54 56 58-60 62 63 65 78-
80 84 | + ⁅Ա⁆բարիմ եղբայր բարձր 8

20 Աբիթան 3-5 7 8 53* 54 56 58-60 62-65 79 80 84 |
Աբիզան 83

21 om 84 | Աբարիմ 3 4 7 58 59 62 63 79 80 |
եղբայր իմ (om 2 79) բարձր omn: cf ln 19

22 Արոն 3-6 8 53 56 58-63 65 78-80 83 84 Արովն 2 57
Արան 7 Արսն 54

23 + թիւ 5

24 om 2 5 6 7 53 54 56 61 65 66 78 83 | ի ծածուկ
3 4 8 58-60 63 79 80 84

25 om omn

26 Ասերովն 2-5 7 8 54 56 58-63 78-80 84 Ասերոն 6
Ասէրոն 56 Ասրովն 83 | իշխանք կամ (om 54 56)
կատարեալք (կատարեալ 59 62) 2-8 53 54 56-63 65
78-80 83 84

27 Ասերովթ 2 Ասերովթ 3-8 53 56-63 65 78-80 83 84
Ասերով 54 | դալիթ } գալիթ 2 4-7 53* 54 56-58 60
63 65 78 80 գալիթ 79 + կամ 53ᶜ

28 Ամուրշացիք 2 3 5 6 61 64 78 Ամուրշացի 54 |
ծաղեալ } չեղեալք (om 2 չեղեալ 57 61 62 66 78 80
չեղեալք 54 58 60 63 80 * գեղեալ 64 ծախեալք 53 ᶜ 56
58) կամ ծաղեալք (ծաղեալ 57 61 66 78 80) 2-8 53 54
56-64 66 78-80 83 84

29 Ամադէկ 2-4 8 54 57-60 62 63 65 66 78-80 83 Ամադեկ
6 | լեզուանոդ 79 լեզուալդ 80 լիգոդ 83

30 Աղովիբեզեկ 5 Աղոնիբեզեկ 7 Աղոնիզեբեկ 54 58 |
չարչարից } 1 60 չարչարիմ 2 արարիչ 56 չարչարի
78 չարչարիչ rel

31 յայնժամ աժժամ 64 + կամ 60 + ժ. 2 | այսք } ազգ
2 78

32   Արկրաքիմ 3   Ամրաքիմ 7   Ակրաթիմ 58   Ակրապիմ 65
      Ակրափիմ 84 | կարիՕ 3 4 8 58 59 62-64 79 80 84
      կարիւք 2
33   Անաբովթ 53 66   Անայթովթ 62
34   Առուէլ 2 3 5 7 54 56 59 60 62 63 65 80 84   Առուէլ
      8 (sic Wutz)   Առուէր 4   Առւէլ 58   Առուէլ 78
      Առուէդ 79 | ընդդեմ} + յաւնել 2-5 7 53c 54
      56 57 59 60 61 63 65 78 79 80 83   + առնել
      8 53* 62 84 | յասոււձոյ 58
      յասոււձոյ 58
35   Աւոդ 2   Աւովթ 3 4 8 53 54 58 59 60 62 63 80 83 84
      Աւաւթ 7   Առոդ 57 | խոսովանեալ 54
36   Աննա }   om 54 | Աննայ 78 84 | արարածոց 53 |
      նոցա } 1 նորա (նորայ 80)   omn
37   Ագոտովս 2-8 53 54 56 58-65   Ագովառս 78-80 83 84
      Ագովոով 57 | ՜րածին}   ՜այրածին 3 | կամ }   om 53
      54 56-65 78-80 83 84
38   Ասկադոն 2-4 6-8 53 54 56-63 65 79 80 84   Ասկադոով
      78   Ասկադովն 5 53   ԱսկադոՀն 83 | կշռեալ 2 4-7 53
      54 56-65 78-80 83 84   կշռեալ 3 (sic Wutz)
39   om 84 | Ակկարովն 5 78 83 | ամրոււթիւն 6
40   Արեսմաթեմ 3 57 66   Արիեսմաթեմ 62   Արեսմմաթեմ 5
      Արիմաթէս 65 79°   Արիմաթիմ 79   Արիսմաթեմ 83 |
      լերինք} + preceding   բարձրուււթիւն կամ 2-8 53 54
      56 57 58 60 61 63 65 66 78 79 80 83 +preceding
      բարձրուււթիււք կամ 8 53   59 62   լերանց 8 59 62

ONA I v A TYPE I : ORDER OF NAMES

No. 65	Nos. 63, 80	No. 54	No. 58	No. 60	No. 56	No. 7	No. 79	
1 Ադամ	1	1	1	1	1	1	1	Adam
2 Ադին	2	2	2	2	2	2	2	Adin
3 Ադին	3	3	3	3	3	3	3	Adin
4 Ադոնիբեզեկ	4	4	4	4	4	4	4	Adonibezek
							Ադոնիրամ	(Adoniram)
							Ադրամելէք	(Adramelēk)
5 Ադդեր	5	5	5	5	5	5	7	Adder
6 Ադրաազար	6	6	6	6	6	6	8	Adraazar
7 Ադրամեղեք	7	7	7	7	7	7		Adramełek'
8 Ադովնայ	8	8	8	8	8	8	9	Adovna
9 Ադովնիայ	9	9	9	9	9	9	10 Ադինա	Adovnia (VL Adina)
10 Ադի	10	10	10	10	10	10	11	Adi
11 Ադոնիէլ	11	11	11	11	11	11	12	Adoniēl
12 Ադադ	12	12	12	12	12	12	13	Adad
						13 Ադամ		(Adam)
13 Ադդա	13	13	13	13	13	14	14	Adda
14 Աբէլ	14	14	14	14	14	15	15	Abēl
15 Աբրահամ	15	15	15	15	15	16	16	Abraham (VL Abram)
16 Աբարամ	16	16	16	16	16	17	17	Abaram (VL Abraham)
17 Աբիմեղեք	17	17	17	17	17	18	18	Abimełek'
18 Աբիթան	18	18	18	18	18	18	19	Abit'an

	col 1	col 2	col 3	col 4	col 5	
19 Աբիգեայ	19	19	19	19	20	20 Abigea
20 Աբիաթար	20	20	20	20	21	21 Abiat'ar
21 Աբեսողոմ	21	21	21	21	22	22 Abēsałom
22 Աբեննէր	22	22	22	22	23	23 Abennēr
23 Աբենեզեր	23	23	23	23	24	24 Abenēzer
24 Աբիդդար	24	24	24	24	25	25 Abiddar
25 Աբեղմայուղայ	25	25	25	25	26	26 Abełmayuła
26 Աբբիայ	26	26	26	26	27	27 Abbia
27 Աբդիու	27	27	27	27	28	28 Abdiu
28 Աբիոն	28	28	28	28	29	29 Abion
29 Աբբանա	29	29	29	29	30	30 Abbana
30 Աբարովթ	Աբարովթ 30	30 Աբարովթ	30Աբարովթ	30Աբարովթ	30Աբարովթ.	31Աբարովթ	31 (Ababovt')
31 Աբիսակ	31	31	31	31	32	32 Abisak
32 Աբբա	32	32	32	32	33Աբբայ	33 Abba (Abbray)
33 Աբրաթ	33	33	33	33	34Աբբայ	34 Abrat' (Abray)
34 Աբանայ	34	34	34	34Աբբ	35	35 Abana
35 Աբեղ 35Աբբաէլ	35Աբբաէլ	35 Աբբէլ	Աբբէլ 35Աբբաէլ	35Աբբաէլ	36Աբբաէլ	36 Abeł (VL Abbaēl)
36 Աբիուրիմ	36	36	36	36	37	37 Abiurim
37 Աբեղբի	37	37	37	37	38	38 Abełbi
38 Աբիուղ	38	38	38	38	39	39 Abiud
39 Աբեղա	39	39	39	39	40	40 Abeła
40 Աբրոտ	40	40	40	40	41	41 Abrot (Abot)

	41 Ազրոկ	41 Ազրոկ	41 Ազրոկ	41 Ազրոկ	41 Ազրոկ	40 Ազարովթ 41 Ազրոկ			
40 Ազար	42	42	42	42	42	42	41	42	(Ababovt')
41 Ազգ							42	43	(Abrok)
42 Ագրամ՚թովն	43	43	43	43	43	43	43	44	Agar
						44 Ազագ			Agag
43 Ազաբոս	44	44	44	44	45	45	44	45	Agṙamt'ovn
44 Արփաքսաթ	45	45	45	45	46	46	45		(Agag)
45 Արաբովթ	46	46	46	46	47	47	46		Agabos
46 Արամ	47	47	47	47	48	48	47		Arp'ak'sat'
47 Արուէլ	48	48	48	48	49	49	48		Arabovt'
48 Արիմաթէմ	49	49	49	49	50	50	49		Aram
49 Արքեղաւոս	50	50	50	50			50		Aruēl
50 Արիսպագոս									Arimat'em

Ark'eławos

Arispagos

46 Ազովր (Azovr)
47 Ազան (Azan)
48 Ազովտոս (Azovtos)
49 Ազայէլ (Azayēl)
50 Ազայզայէլ (Azayzayēl)

ONA I v B TYPE II : ORDER OF NAMES

No. 5	No. 57	No. 61	No. 78	No. 83	
1 Ադամ	1	1	1	1	Adam
2 Աբէլ	2	2	2	2	Abēl
3 Ադին	3	3	3 Ադէ	3	Adin (Adē)
4 Արփաքսադ	4	4	4	4	Arp'ak'sad
5 Ասուր	5	5	5	5	Asur
6 Աբրամ	6 Աբրաամ	6 Աբրահամ	6	6	Abram (VL Abraham)
7 Աբրաամ	7	7	7	7	Abraam
8 Ագար	8	8	8		Agar
9 Աւնան	9	9	9	8	Awnan
10 Ամարփաղ	10	10	10 Ամրափաղ	9	Amarp'ał (VL Amra-p'ał)
11 Աբիմելէք	11	11	11	10	Abimelek'
12 Ամմովն	12	12	12	11 Ամնոն	Ammovn (Amnon)
13 Ասեր	13	12	13	12	Aser
		13 Աբիմելիք			(Abimelik')
14 Արամ	14	14	14	13	Aram
				14 Ագար	Agar
15 Ամինադաբ	15	15	15	15	Aminadab
16 Ամրամ	16	16	16	16	Amram
17 Ահարովն	17	17	17	17	Aharovn
18 Աբիթան	18	18		18	Abit'an
19 Աբիդար	19 Աբիդար	19 Աբիդար			(Abidar)

Armenian entry	col 1	col 2	col 3	col 4	Transliteration
					(Aharon)
19 Ասերովթ	20	20			Aserovt'
					(Adin)
20 Աբիրամ	21	21	21 Աբիրամ	19	Ak'iram (Abiram)
21 Ասերովն	22	22	22	20	Aserovn
				21 Ասրովն	(Asrovn)
22 Ամուրհաչացիք	23	23	23	22	Amurhac'ik'
23 Ամաղեկ	24	24	24	23	Amałek
24 Ադովնիբեզեկ	25	25	25	24	Adovnibezek
25 Ազան	26	26	26	25	Azan
26 Ակրաբիմ	27	27	27	26	Akrabim
27 Անաթովթ	28	28	28	27	Anat'ovt'
28 Արուէլ	29 Արուէր	29 Արուէր	29 Արուէր	28 Արուէր	Aruēl (VL Aruēr)
29 Աւովդ	30 Արոդ	30 Արոդ	30 Արոդ	29	Awovd (Abod)
30 Աննա	31	31	31	30	Anna
	32 Ասկարոն	32 Ասկարոն	32 Ասկարոն		(Askał n)
31 Ազովտոս	33	33	33	31	Azovtos
32 Ասկաղովն	34	34	34	32	Askałovn
33 Ակկարովն	34	35	34		Akkarovn
34 Արիմմաթեմ	35	35	35	33	Arimmat'em
				34 Ակկարոն	(Akkaron)
35 Ասերովք	36 Ասերովթ	36 Ասերովթ	36 Ասերովթ	35	Ak'erovk' (VL Ak'er-ovt')
36 Աքիմելեք	37	37	37	36	Ak'imelek'

					English
37 Աբիաթար				37	Abiat'ar
38 Ամատտարա	38	38		38	Amattara
39 Աբիգեա	39	39 Աշիթեա	38	39	Abigea (VL Abit'ea)
40 Անրուս	40 Արուս	40 Արուս	39	40	Ank'us (VL Ak'us)
			40		(Abia)
41 Այենովդր	41 Այենովդ	41 Այենովկ	41 Արուս	41	Ayendovr (VLL Ayenovd
			42 Աբիա		Ayenovg)
42 Աբեսադովմ	42	42	43 Այենովք	42	Abesałovm
43 Աբիտոփել	43	43	44	43	Ak'itop'el
44 Աբիմաաս	44	44	45	44	Ak'imaas
45 Աբեններ	45	45	46	45	Abenner
46 Ասաէլ	46	46	47	46	Asael
47 Ամեսսաի	47	47	48	47	Amessai
48 Աբենեզեր	48	48	49	48	Abenezer
49 Ասափ	49	49	50	49	Asap'
50 Աեըուիա	50	50		50	Aleluia
50 Ասրին					(Astin)

No. 59		No. 62	
1	Ադամ	1	Adam
2	Ադային	2	Adayin
3	Ադադ	3	Adad
4	Ադդա	4	Adda
5	Ադին	5	Adin
6	Ադի	6	Adi
7	Ադոնիբեզեկ	7	Adonibezek
8	Ադոնա	8	Adona
9	Ադոնիա	9	Adonia
10	Ադոնիէլ	10	Adoniēl
11	Ադդեր	11	Adder
12	Ադրազար	12	Adrazar
13	Ադրամելէք	13	Adramelēk'
14	Աբէդ	14	Abēɫ
15	Աբէդմայուզա	15	Abēlmayuza
16	Աբեդա	16	Abeɫa
17	Աբենէր	17	Abenēr
18	Աբենեզեր	18 Աբենեզ	Abenezer (VL Abenez)
19	Աբեդդար	19	Abeddar
20	Աբէլփի		Abēlpʻi
21	Աբրամ	21	Abram
22	Աբրաամ	22	Abraam
23	Աբրոկ	23	Abrok
24	Աբիմելէք	24	Abimelēk'
25	Աբիթան	25	Abit'an
26	Աբիաթար	26	Abiat'ar
27	Աբիգեայ	27	Abigea
28	Աբիսողոմ	28	Abisoɫom
29	Աբիսակ	29	Abisak
30	Աբբիայ	30	Abbia
31	Աբբանայ	31	Abbana
32	Աբբա	32 Աբբիայ	Abba (VL Abbia)
		33 Աբբայէլ	(Abbayēl)
33	Աբանա	34	Abana
34	Աբաբովթ	35	Ababovt'

35	Աբիոն	36	Abion
36	Աբիւրիմ	37	Abiurim
37	Աբիուդ	38	Abiud
38	Աբդիւ	39	Abdiu
39	Աբոտ	40	Abot
40	Ազար	41	Agar
41	Ազաբոս	42	Agabos
42	Ազրամբովն	43	Agṙambovn
43	Ազագ	44	Agag
44	Արփաքսաթ	45	Arp'ak'sat'
45	Արաբովթ	46	Arabovt'
46	Արամ	47	Aram
47	Արամաթի	48	Aramat'i
48	Արաբիայ	49	Arabia
49	Արա	50	Ara
50	Արրա		Arra

No. 64

No. 64

1	Աբբա	35	Ագազ
2	Աբբանայ	36	Ագասութիւնք
3	Աբբոր	37	Ագարսա
4	Աբբայէլ	38	Ագապոս
5	Աբեներ	39	Ագդէն
6	Աբբոկ	40	Ագորանք
7	Աբդլմսիհ	41	Ագոն
8	Աբդիու	42	Ագուո
9	Աբեղա	43	Ագունիա
10	Աբբեթղարա	44	Ագոո
11	Աբեղբի	45	Ագովր
12	Աբենեզէր	46	Աղամ
13	Աբէլ	47	Աղադ
14	Աբէլմաուլայ	48	Աղդէր
15	Աբիոն	49	Աղղա
16	Աբիմելէք	50	Աղին
17	Աբիդան		
18	Աբիդար		
19	Աբիդա		
20	Աբիսողմ		
21	Աբիա		
22	Աբիուրիմ		
23	Աբիութ		
24	Աբոդ		
25	Աբրայ		
26	Աբրամ		
27	Աբրասմ		
28	Աբրաթ		
29	Ագապէն		
30	Ագապ		
31	Ագաթանգեղոս		
32	Ագարակք		
33	Ագաթեմովթ		
34	Ագանեղ		

1	Abba	35	Agag̃
2	Abbana	36	Agasut'iwnk'
3	Abbor	37	Agarsa
4	Abbayēl	38	Agabos
5	Abenēr	39	Agdēn
6	Abbok	40	Agorank'
7	Abdlmsih	41	Agon
8	Abdiu	42	Aguṙ
9	Abeła	43	Agunia
10	Abbedt'ara	44	Agoṙ
11	Abełbi	45	Agovr
12	Abenezēr	46	Adam
13	Abeł	47	Adad
14	Abēlmaula	48	Addēr
15	Abion	49	Adda
16	Abimelēk'	50	Adin
17	Abidan		
18	Abidar		
19	Abida		
20	Abisołom		
21	Abia		
22	Abiurim		
23	Abiut'		
24	Abod		
25	Abra		
26	Abram		
27	Abraam		
28	Abrat'		
29	Agapēn		
30	Agap		
31	Agat'angełos		
32	Agarakk'		
33	Agat'ṙemovt'		
34	Aganel		

No. 53

1A	{Աբաբովթ}	34	Ադդեր
1	Աբանայ	35	Ադի
2	Աբբայ	35	{Ադէն}
3	Աբբանայ	36	Ադին
4	Աբբայէլ	37	Ադին
4A	{Աբբէդ }	38	Ադ{դ}ին
5	Աբբիա	39	Ադին
6	Աբդիու	40	Ադոնիբեզեկ
7	Աբեդդար{այ}	41	Ադովնայ
8	Աբեդայ	42	Ադովնիայ
9	Աբէդ	43	Ադովնիէլ
10	Աբէդբի	44	Ադրայագար
11	Աբէդմայուդայ	45	Ադրամելէք
12	Աբենեզեր	46	Ազազայէլ
13	Աբեննէր	47	Ազայէլ
14	Աբէսողոմ	48	Ազան
15	Աբիաթար	49	Ազապարայ
16	Աբիայ	50	Ազար
17	Աբիդեա		
18	Աբիթան		
19	Աբիմեդէք		
20	Աբիոն		
21	Աբիուդ		
22	Աբիուրիմ		
23	Աբիսակ		
24	Աբոտ		
25	Աբրահամ		
26	Աբրաթ		
27	Աբրամ		
27A	{Աբրոկ}		
28	Ազաբոս		
29	Ազազ		
30	Ազարոտմթովն		
31	Ազար		
32	Ադամ		
33	Ադդա		

1A {Ababovt'}	33 Adda
1 Abana	34 Addēr
2 Abba	35 Adi
3 Abbana	35A {Adēn}
4 Abbayēl	36 Adin
4A {Abbeł}	37 Adin
5 Abbia	38 Ad{d}in
6 Abdiu	39 Adin
7 Abeddar{a}	40 Adonibezak
8 Abeła	41 Adovna
9 Abēł	42 Adovnia
10 Abēłbi	43 Adovniēl
11 Abēłmayuła	44 Adrayazar
12 Abenezer	45 Adramelēk'
13 Abennēr	46 Azazayēl
14 Abēsołom	47 Azayēl
15 Abiat'ar	48 Azan
16 Abia	49 Azapara
17 Abidea	50 Azar
18 Abit'an	
19 Abimełēk'	
20 Abion	
21 Abiud	
22 Abiurim	
23 Abisak	
24 Abot	
25 Abraham	
26 Abrat'	
27 Abram	
27A {Abrok}	
28 Agabos	
29 Agag	
30 Agabŕamt'ovn	
31 Agar	
32 Adam	

ONA I v F TYPE VI : ORDER OF NAMES

No. 84

No. 84

1 Ադամ
2 Ադին
3 Ադոնիբեզեկ
4 Ադոնիրամ
5 Ադոնա
6 Ադոնիէլ
7 Ադոնիայ
8 Ադադ
9 Ադդայ
10 Ադդեր
11 Ադրամէլիք
12 Ադրայազար
13 Աբբա
14 Աբբիայ
15 Աբբանայ
16 Աբբայէլ
17 Աբանայ
18 Աբարովթ
19 Աբդիու
20 Աբանէր
21 Աբենեզեր
22 Աբելմայուսայ
23 Աբեդդար
24 Աբեդայ
25 Աբէլ
26 Աբէսողոմ
27 Աբէլբի
28 Աբիաթր
29 Աբիգեայ
30 Աբիթան
31 Աբիմէլէք
32 Աբին
33 Աբիւղ
34 Աբիւրիմ
35 Աբիսակ

36 Արոտ
37 Աբրամ
38 Աբրաամ
39 Աբրայ
40 Աբրոկ
41 Ազար
42 Ազատմթովն
43 Ազարոս
44 Ազովր
45 Ազան
46 Ազայէլ
47 Ազազայէլ
48 Ազար
49 Ազարիայ
50 [   ]

1 Adam	36 Abot
2 Adin	37 Abram
3 Adonibezek	38 Abraam
4 Adoniram	39 Abra
5 Adona	40 Abrok
6 Adoniēl	41 Agar
7 Adonia	42 Agařmt'ovn
8 Adad	43 Agabos
9 Adda	44 Agovr
10 Adder	45 Azan
11 Adramēlik'	46 Azayēl
12 Adrayazar	47 Azazayēl
13 Abba	48 Azar
14 Abbia	49 Azaria
15 Abbana	50 [ ]
16 Abbayēl	
17 Abana	
18 Ababovt'	
19 Abdiu	
20 Abanēr	
21 Abenezer	
22 Abelmayusa	
23 Abeddar	
24 Abeła	
25 Abēl	
26 Abēsołom	
27 Abēlbi	
28 Abiat'ar	
29 Abigea	
30 Abit'an	
31 Abimēlēk'	
32 Abion	
33 Abiud	
34 Abiurim	
35 Abisak	

III

ONA   III

Յերրայեցւոց բանից մնացեալք են քանզի յառաջագոյն ոչ
ունեցաք ի մտի շարադրել ընդ նմին բանի:

1	Աբբայ.	Հայր, ասորւոց է բառս:
2	Աբարիմ.	անցք կամ անցանօղք:
3	Աբդեմելեք.	ծառայ թագաւորի:
4	Աբդենագո.	ծառայ պայծառութեան:
5	Աբդիաս.	ծառայ տեառն:
6	Աբդոն.	ծառայ:
7	Աբեդ.	ի ծեռն ալիֆի, Հեծման քաղաք. իսկ ի ծեռն Հէի ներ սկզբան, ունայնութիւն, որդի Ադամայ: Այս ըստ դադմատացւոց, իսկ ի մերս,
8	Աբէդ.	յաստուծոյ տուեալ մարգարէութիւն կամ տեսանելի կամ գոլորշի սգոյ կամ գուծ վերամբերեալ կամ երկիր պտղաբեր:
9	Աբէսաղոմ.	Հայր խաղաղութեան:
10	Աբիա.	Հայր տեառն:
11	Աբիաթար.	Հայր բարձրագոյ:
12	Աբիգայիլ.	Հայր ցնծութեան:
13	Աբիգայ.	Հօր իմոյ յայտնութիւն:
14	Աբիմելեք.	Հայր թագաւոր կամ Հօր իմոյ արքայու-թիւն:
15	Ամինադաբ.	Հայր Հարսանեաց:

(These) are those remaining of the Hebrew Words, for
previously we did not intend to arrange them with the
same vocabulary.

1   Abbay,   father, this is a Syriac word.

2   Abarim,   passage, or passers.

3   Abdemelek',   servant of king.

4   Abdenagō,   servant of brilliance.

5   Abdias,   servant of lord.

6   Abdōn,   servant.

7   Abel,   with Alif, city of wailing; but with

                        Hē at the beginning, nothingness,

                        son of Adam. This is according to

                        the Dalmatians, but in our

                        (tradition),

8   Abel,   prophecy given by God or visible or

                        vapour of mourning or elevated pity

                        or fruitful earth.

9   Abēsalom,   father of peace.

10 Abia,   father of lord.

11 Abiat'ar,   sublime father.

12 Abigayil,   father of rejoicing.

13 Abika,   my father's revelation.

14 Abimelēk',   father king or my father's kingdom.

15 Aminadab,   father of wedding.

16   Աբիսակ.   Հոր ազիտութիւն կամ Հոր իմոյ

                        աւետիք:

17   Աբներ.   Հոր ճրագ:

18   Աբեներ.   Հայր կամ որդի ճրագ{ի}:

19   Աբրա.   ադախին, յունաց է բառ:

20   Աբրամ.   Հայր վերամբարձ կամ մեծարգոյ:

1   Աբբա | ասրրոց}   սիրացւոց | բառ   2   անցաւորք
3   Արղեմեդեք   4   Արդենագով | ծառա   5   Աբիդաս
7   Աբէդ | ի ձեռն 1°---իսկ }   om | Հէի }   + որ է
Հաբէդ | սկզբանն | այս---մերս }   om   8   om
9   Աբիսապոմ   13   Աբիգալ   14   Աբիմեդեք |
կամ Հոր իմոյ արքայութիւն }   om   15   Հարսանաւոր
16   Աբիսագ | կամ---աւետիք}   om   17   Աբներ
18   om   19   յունական   20   կամ մեծարգոյ }   om

16   Abisak,   father's ignorance or my father's

                 gospel.

17   Abner,   father's candle.

18   Abener,   candle's father or son.

19   Abra,   maid-servant, it is a Greek word.

20   Abram,   exalted or revered father.

ln 1   MS 9 ln 2: Ona V ln 2: MS 9 is that whose text
        is printed by Wutz.

ln 2   MS 9 ln 1, Ona V ln 3.

ln 3   MS 9 ln 4, Ona V ln 5.

ln 4   MS 9 ln 3, Ona V ln 8.

ln 5   MS 9 ln 15: The form in MS 9 is somewhat corrupt,
        Աբիդաս   "Abidas", and has, secondarily been
        placed lower in the alphabetical order. Ona V
        ln 4 has "Abdiu" with this etymology.

ln 6   MS 9 ln 6, Ona V ln 6.

ln 7   The words: with "Alif" city of weeping, but, are
        omitted by MS 9 ln 9. This etymology is clearly
        behind that of Ona V ln 9. See also Ona V ln 10.

        The introduction of "our tradition" for the etymo-
        logy of Abel is the insertion of the entry for
        Abel from Ona I (see Ona I, iv, ln 2, supra).
        This is not reflected in MS 9 or in Ona V.
        "Dalmatians" here designates the Latins.

ln 9   MS 9 ln 18, Ona V ln 12.

ln 10   MS 9 ln 10, Ona V ln 13.

ln 11   MS 9 ln 11, Ona V ln 14 different wording.

ln 12   MS 9 ln 12. In Ona V ln 14 the same etymology
        occurs with the name "Abigea".

ln 13   The form "Abigal" of MS 9 ln 13 seems preferable.
        Omitted by Ona V.

ln 14   MS 9 ln 16, Ona V ln 19: The second of the two
        etymologies does not occur in either of these
        sources. It is drawn from Ona I ln 11.

ln 15   Cf. MS 9 ln 19.   Contrast Ona V ln 17 and
         note there.

ln 16   MS 9 ln 17, Ona V ln 19.   The second meaning
         is to be found in Ona II ln 11.

lns 17-18 MS 9 ln 19 = ln 17.   MS 9 omits ln 18.   In
         Ona V ln 11 we read "Abenner, father's candle".
         Ln 18 corresponds to Ona I ln 51.

ln 19   MS 9 ln 21, Ona V ln 20.

ln 20   MS 9 ln 22, Ona V ln 22.   "And revered"   occurs
         in Ona I ln 6.

IV

ONA IV

Այլ բառ եբրայեցւոց է ի վերայ այթուբենից ըստ
անուանակոչութեանց.

1 (1) (Ա)դամ. երկիր կամ կոյս:

2 (2) Աբէլ. Աստուծոյ տրւեալ մարգարէութիւն:

3 (4) Արփաքսադ. մաքրութիւն տեսանելի:

4 (7) Աբրահամ. հայր ազգաց:

5 (11) Աբիմելէք, հոր իմոյ արքայութիւն:

6 (16) Ամինադաբ. ազգ ցանկալի:

7 (19) Ահարոն. ահա լեառն կամ հոգի կամ
                 բան:

8 (28) Ամուրհացիք. չեղեալ կամ ծաղեալ:

9 (29) Ամաղէկ. ազգ լեզուող:

10 (33) Անաքովթ. պատասխանի:

11 (36) Աննայ. արարած նորայ:

12 (48) Աքիսողոմ. հայր խաղաղութեան:

13 (40) Արիմաթեմ. բարձրութիւնք կամ լերինք:

14 (49) Ակիտաբէլ. եղբօր զլորուն:

15 (56) Ալէլուհայ. աւրհնեցէք զտէր կամ գովեցէք զաս-
                    տուած:

16 (60) Ամովսիայ. յազգէ հաւատարմէն:

17 (65) Ազագիէլ. տեսիլ աստուծոյ:

18 (76) Աքազ. զօրութիւն:

19 (72) Ասուր. խորհուրդ սուրբ:

20 (74) Ադոնա. տէր:

21 (75) Ադոնիայ. տերանց տէր:

Another vocabulary of the Hebrews is based upon the alphabet according to the names.

1 (1)   Adam,   earth or virgin.

2 (2)   Abēl   prophecy given from God.

3 (4)   Arp'ak'sad, visible cleanliness.

4 (7)   Abraham   father of nations.

5 (11) Abimelēk',   my father's kingdom.

6 (16) Aminadab,   desirable nation.

7 (19) Aharon,   behold a mountain or a spirit or a
                     word.

8 (28) Amurhac'ik', not having been or having mocked.

9 (29) Amałek,   licking nation.

10 (33) Anabovt',   answer.

11 (36) Anna,   his (her) creation.

12 (48) Abisołom,   father of peace.

13 (40) Arimat'em,   elevations or mountains.

14 (49) Akidabēl,   brother's ruin.

15 (56) Alēluia,   bless the Lord or praise God.

16 (60) Amovsia,   from the faithful people.

17 (65) Azaziēl,   vision of God.

18 (76) Akaaz,   power.

19 (72) Asur,   holy thought.

20 (74) Adona,   Lord.

21 (75) Adonia,   Lord of lords.

22 (78) Անանիայ.   շնորհք:

23 (79) Ազարիայ.   արձակումն:

24 (82) Աւգոստոս.   տոն ոզի ստացանք:

25 (85) Անդրիաս.   ազգի սիրելի կամ վայելուչ:

26 (87) Ամէն.   եղիցի կամ ճշմարտութիւն:

27 (93) Աբբա.   հայր հօր:

28 (69) Ամբակում.   հայր յարուցանող կամ արդարացեալ:

29 (28) Անաձ.   պատգամ.

30 (60) Ամասիայ.   յազգէ հաւատարիմ:

31 (էջ 864) Ագբակ.   մուկ:

32   արգաւանդ.   երկիր բերող կամ պարարտ:

33   արգ<ա>սաւոր.   գովեալ:

34   արդարեւ.   է այսպէս:

35   արւարձան.   ոտար կամ այլազգի:

36   անուրջ.   ծածուկ կամ երազ:

37   անընդհատ.   միակարգ կամ ստէպ ստէպ:

38   անչրպետ.   անչատող:

39   առհաւատչեա.   գրաւական ազգական:

40   ապաշաւիլ.   փոշեմանիլ:

41   անդրադարձումն. յետ դառնալ կամ երկու

                     դիմաց կարդալ. որ է

                     այսպէս սողոս:

22 (78) Anania,   grace.

23 (79) Azaria,   deliverance.

24 (82) Awgōstos,   we received a feast soul

                     (<u>corr. for</u> celebrating).

25 (85) Andrias,   of a beloved nation or delightful.

26 (87) Amēn,   let it be or truth.

27 (93) Abba,   father's father.

28 (69) Ambakum,   resurrecting father or righteous.

29 (23) Aṙac,   command.

30 (60) Amasia,   from a faithful people.

31(p.864n) Agbak,   mouse.

32   <u>argawand</u>,   fruitful earth or rich.

33   <u>arg(a)ɔawor</u>, praised.

34   <u>ardarew</u>,   it is thus.

35   <u>aruarjan</u>,   strange or alien.

36   <u>anurǰ</u>,   secret or quick.

37   <u>anəndhat</u>,   of single order or very often.

38   <u>anǰrpet</u>,   separator.

39   <u>aṙhawatč'ea</u>, pledge, relative.

40   <u>apašawil</u>,   repent.

41   <u>andradarjumn</u>, to turn back or to set in two

                     directions.

                     which is thus ⌐<u>unknown word</u>⌐.

42 (130) Թաբելոն. փոփոխումն կամ խոովութիւն:

43 (134) Բենիամին. որդի վշտաց կամ սգոյ:

44 (173) Բեթսափիդայ. տուն ողորմութեան:

45 (168) Բէլ. այլապիսի աստուած:

46 (182) Բելիար. ապատամբ:

47 (167) Բոսոր. կարմրութիւն մարմնոց:

48 (141) Բեսելիէլ. ի հովանի աստուծոյ:

49 (139) Բերսաբէ. դուստր լցեալ կամ զօրաւոր:

50 (169) Բաղտասար. անկտութիւն երանութեան:

51 (171) Բարդուղիմէոս. որդիք ստոյք աստուծոյ:

52 (173) Բեղսայիդայ. տուն ողորմութեան:

53 (176) Բենգեերուդ. դել պարատու կամ իշխան

դիւաց:

54 (177) Բաննաբաս. որդի մխիթարութեան:

55 (153) Բահադ. պատրիչ:

56 (196) Բերովբա. ճանճ:

57 (156) Բեթլեհեմ. տուն հացի կամ տուն մսի:

42 (130) Babelon,   exchange or confusion.

43 (134) Beniamin,   son of pains or of sorrow.

44 (173) Bet'saida,   house of mercy.

45 (160) Bel,   different god.

46 (182) Beliar,   rebellion.

47 (167) Bosor,   redness of bodies.

48 (141) Beseliel,   in the shade of God.

49 (139) Bersabē,   full daughter or powerful.

50 (169) Baltasar,   undeceitfulness of benediction.

51 (171) Baldulimēos,   assured sons of God.

52 (173) Bedsayida,   house of mercy.

53 (176) Belzebul,   inclusive demon or prince of

                            demons.

54 (177) Barnabas,   son of pity.

55 (153) Bahal,   seducer.

56 (196) Berovba,   fly.

57 (156) Bet'lēhem,   house of bread or house of meat.

V

ONA V

300բ 1 Մեկնութիւն անուանց յեբրայեցւոց

 լեզուէ ի հայ բարբառ

Աբբայ. Հայր ասորդ է բառ։

Աբբարիմ. անցք կամ անցօրք։

Աբդիու. ծառայ տեառն։

5 Աբդիմելէք. ծառայ արքայի։

Աբդոն. ծառայ։

Աբեդդար. ծառայ մարդոյ։

Աբեդնագով. ծառայ պայծառութեան։

Աբէլ. սուգ կամ լալումն կամ քաղաք։

10 Աբէլ. ունայնութիւն որդի ադամայ։

Աբեններ. Հոր ճրագ։

Աբէսողոմ. Հայր խաղաղութեան։

Աբիայ. Հայր տեառն։

Աբիաթար. Հայր զերագոյն։

15 Աբիգեա. Հայր ցնծութեան։

Աբիմէլէք. Հայր թագաւոր։

Աբինադաբ. Հայր կամաւոր։

Աբեսսեա. ցամաք կամ տրտմութիւն։

Աբիսակ. Հոր անզիտութիւն։

20 Աբրա. ադախին յունաց է բառ։

Աբրամ. Հայր բազմութեան։

Աբրամ. Հայր վերամբարձ։

Ագաբ. մարախ։

Ագագ. տանիս։

300v 1   Interpretation of Names from the Hebrew

             Tongue into the Armenian Language

Abba ,	father, it is a Syriac word.
Abbarim,	passage or passers.
Abdiu,	servant of lord.
5 Abdimelēk',	servant of king.
Abdon,	servant.
Abeddar,	servant of man.
Abednagov,	servant of brilliance.
Abēl,	mourning, or weeping, or city.
10 Abēl,	nothingness, son of Adam.
Abenner,	father's candle.
Abēsoɬom,	father of peace.
Abia,	father of lord.
Abiat'ar,	sublime father.
15 Abigea,	father of rejoicing.
Abimēlēk',	father king.
Abinadab,	willing father.
Abessea,	dry land, or sadness.
Abisak,	father's ignorance.
20 Abra,	maid-servant, it is a Greek word.
Abraam,	father of multitude.
Abram,	exalted father.
Agab,	locust.
Agag,	roof.

25 Ազան.   նեղութիւն:/

301ա   Ագար.   պանդուխտ:

Ադամ.   մարդ երկրային կամ կարմիր:

Ադոնա.   տէր:

Ադոնայի.   տեարք իմ:

30 Ադունիա.   տիրող կամ տէր:

Ազարիա.   օգնութիւն տեառն:

Ագովտոս.   կողոպուտ:

Ագովր.   օգնական:

Աթադիա.   ժամանակ տեառն:

35 Ակկարոն.   ամլութիւն:

Ահարոն.   լեառն կամ լեննային:

Ահովտ.   գովասանող:

Աղեղուիայ.   աւրհնեցէք զտէր:

Աղեկսանդեր.   քաջ օգնական:

40 Աղեկսանդրիայ.   եբրա<յերէն> նոյ որ է հուն:

Ամաղէք.   թագաւոր:

Ամամ.   մայր կամ երկիւղ նոցա:

Աման.   խռովեցուցանող:

Ամանայ.   հաւատ կամ ճշմարտութիւն:

45 Ամբակում.   ողբասէր:

Ամրի.   դառն կամ զոր այն կամ

տերութիւն:

Ամասիա.   քաջ կամ զօրեղ:

Ամեսայի.   ժողովրդեան պարգեւ:

25	Agan,	affliction./
301r	Agar,	sojourner.
	Adam,	earthly man, or red.
	Adona,	lord.
	Adonayi,	my lords.
30	Adonia,	ruler or lord.
	Azaria,	lord's help.
	Azovtcs,	booty.
	Azovr,	helpful.
	At'aɫia,	lord's time.
35	Akkaron,	sterility.
	Aharon,	mountain, or mountainous.
	Ahovt,	praiser.
	Aɫēɫuia,	praise the Lord.
	Aɫeksandēr,	brave, helpful.
40	Aɫeksantria,	Hebr<ew> Noy which is cruel.
	Amaɫēk',	king.
	Amam,	mother, or their fear.
	Aman,	disturber.
	Amana,	faith, or truth.
45	Ambakum,	love of laments.
	Amri,	bitter, or that force, or mastery.
	Amasia,	brave, or powerful.
	Amesayi,	people's gift.

Ամէն.	եղիցի կամ հաստատուն լիցի:

50 Ամինադաբ.	ժողովուրդ կամաւոր:
Ամմոն.	ժռովուրդ նորա:
Ամոն.	հաւատարիմ:
Ամովս.	զօրեղ կամ քաջ կամ հայրն / եսայեա է:

301բ

Ամովս.	ծանրացեալ, մարգարէն է:
55 Ամուրհացի.	դառն կամ ապստամբք:
Անանիա.	ամպ տեառն:
Անաթովթ.	պատասխանի կամ երգ:
Անզեաս.	ուրախարար:
Անդրեաս.	քաջազոյն:
60 Աննա.	ցանկալի կամ ողորմած:
Անտիոքիա.	կառք:
Ապողոս.	ճարտար կամ խորհրդական:
Ասեր.	որդի յակոբայ աւրհնութիւն կամ երանութիւն:
Ասթինէ.	ըմպող:
65 Ասուր.	որոգայթ վերանող կամ երանելի:
Ասվերուս.	իշխան կամ գլուխ:
Ասարովթ.	հօտք կամ ստացուածք:
Ասքա.	զարդարեալ:

	Amēn,	let it be, or let it be estab-lished.
50	Aminadab,	willing people.
	Ammon,	his people.
	Amon,	faithful.
301v	Amovs,	powerful, or brave, or the father/of Isaiah.
	Amovs,	having become heavy, it is the prophet.
55	Amurhac'i,	bitter, or rebellion.
	Anania,	lord's cloud.
	Anat'ovt',	reply, or song.
	Angēas,	joyous.
	Andrēas,	most brave.
60	Anna,	desirable, or merciful.
	Antiok'ia,	chariot.
	Apolos,	skillful or mysterious.
	Aser,	son of Jacob; blessing or felicity.
	Ast'inē,	drinker.
65	Asur,	ambush, ascender, or felicitous.
	Asverus,	ruler, or head.
	Astarovt,	flocks, or possessions.
	Ask'a,	having decorated.

Արաբացիք.　　　երեկեանք:

70 Արաբացիք.　　　երրայեցերէն սաքայ որ է դար-
　　　　　　　　　　　　　　　　　　ծումն:

Արամ.　　　　　թարձրութիւն:

Արարատ.　　　　անէծք դողութեան:

Արբոկ.　　　　　չորք:

Արի ⊲ϩ ⊳պագոս.　　բլուր մարտի:

75 Արոն.　　　　　տապանակ կամ երգ:

Արտաքսեր< ք >սէս. ՛ճառագայթ կամ անէծք:

Արփաքսաթ.　　　թժշկող:

302ք　Աբայեաք.　　　եղբայր / ՛որ:

Աքիմելէք.　　　եղբայր իմ արքայ:

80 Աքայիա.　　　վիշտ կամ նեղութիւն:

Աքագ.　　　　　ըմբոնող կամ ստացող:

Աքիտոփէլ.　　　եղբայր բարութեան:

Բաքէլ.　　　　　խառնակութիւն կամ ամօթ:

Բաթուէլ.　　　　որդի աստուծոյ:

85 Բաՙած.　　　　կուրք կամ տիրող:

Բ⊔ ɭɭ ⊔.　　　　նաժիշտ ռաքելա

　　　　　　　　　ծերացեալ կամ զարՙուրեալ:

Բաղամ.　　　　՛նութիւն ժողովրդեան:

Բաղակ.　　　　ալերող:

Բալլա.　　　　 քաղաք ընկլուզող կամ ալերող:

90 Բանեա.　　　　որդի տեառն:

Բաներեգէս.　　　որդիք որոտման:

	Arabac'ik',	belonging to yesterday.
70	Arabac'ik',	Hebrew Sabay, which is return.
	Aram,	height.
	Ararat,	curses of trembling.
	Arbok,	four.
	Ari⟨o⟩pagos,	hill of battle.
75	Aron,	ark, or song.
	Ardak'ser⟨k'⟩sēs,	ray, or curse.
	Arp'ak'sat',	healer.

302r

	Ak'ayeab,	father's/brother.
	Ak'imelēk',	my brother king.
80	Ak'ayia,	sorrow, or affliction.
	Ak'az,	seizer, or possessor.
	Ak'itop'ēl,	brother of goodness.
	Babēl,	confusion, or shame.
	Bat'uēl,	son of God.
85	Bahał,	idol or master.
	Balla,	Rachel's maid-servant;
		aged, or amazed.
	Bałaam,	people's antiquity.
	Bałak,	destroyer.
	Balla,	city, swallower, or destroyer.
90	Banea,	lord's son.
	Banereges,	thunder's sons.

	Բատոս.	*շափ Հալոդականաց:*
	Բարակ.	*փայլական:*
	Բարիովնա.	*որդի աղաւնոյ:*
95	*Բարսաբայ.*	*որդի դարձման:*
	Բառնաբաս.	*որդի մխիթարութեան:*
	Բարրուք.	*աւրհնեալ:*
	Բարթիմէոս.	*որդի կոյր:*
	Բէելզեբուդ.	*կուռք ճանճիկ:*
100	*Բեզեկ.*	*փայլական կամ խիստ:*
	Բեթանիա.	*տուն հնազանդութեան կամ*
		նեղութեան:
	Բեթբաթայ.	*տուն անցից:*
302բ	*Բեթաւան./*	*տուն ունայնութեան:*
	Բեթէլ.	*տուն աստուծոյ:*
105	*Բեթէր.*	*բաժանումն:*
	Բեթդահէմ.	*տուն Հացի:*
	Բերսաբէ.	*դուստր երդման:*
	Բեթսաբէէ.	*տուն երդման:*
	Բեթսամիս.	*տուն արեգական:*
110	*Բեթսայիդայ.*	*տուն պտղոց.*
	Բեթբաբէ.	*տուն բերանոյ Հովտաց:*
	Բեթբաքովր.	*տուն անդնդոց:*
	Բելիար.	*նենգաւոր կամ առանց լծոյ:*
	Բելփեբովր.	*կուռք անդնդոց:*

	Batos,	measure of liquids.
	Barak,	ray.
	Bariovna,	dove's son.
95	Barsaba,	son of return.
	Barnabas,	son of mercy.
	Baruk',	blessed.
	Bartimēos,	blind son.
	Bēelzebuł,	idol fly.
100	Bezek,	ray, or difficult.
	Bet'ania,	house of obedience or of affliction.
	Bet'abat'a,	house of passings./
302v	Bet'awan,	house of inutility.
	Bet'ēl,	house of God.
105	Bet'ēr,	division.
	Bet'łahem,	house of bread.
	Bersabē,	oath's daughter.
	Bet'sabēē,	oath's house.
	Bet'samiws,	sun's house.
110	Bet'sayida,	house of fruit.
	Bet'bak'ē,	house of mouth of valley.
	Bet'bak'ovr,	house of abyss.
	Beliar,	treacherous, or without yoke
	Belp'ek'ovr,	idol of abyss.

115　Բեհմովթ.　　　　խաշինք կամ շորքոտանիք:

　　　Բենիամին.　　　　որդի աջոյ:

　　　Բենոնի.　　　　　որդի վշտաց իմոց:

　　　Բետուէլ.　　　　կոյս:

　　　Բերա.　　　　　չրհոր:

120　Բերսաբէէ.　　　chrhor երդման:

　　　Բեթդագոն.　　　տուն ցորենւոյ:

　　　Բէլ.　　　　　հնացեալ:

　　　Բելա.　　　　ընկլուզող կամ աւերող:

　　　Բոյոս.　　　　ի զօրութեան:

125　Բոսովր.　　　ամրութիւն:

　　　Բրեսիթ.　　　առաջին գիրք օրինաց

　　　　　　　　　այսպէս անուանի:

　　　Գաբայեա.　　բլուր:

　　　Գաբայադ.　　ընկեցումն: /

303ա　Գաբրիէլ.　　այր աստուած կամ աստուծոյ:

130　Գաթ.　　　　երանելի կամ արագահաս:

　　　Գաղգադ.　　երանութիւն երանութեան կամ

　　　　　　　　　արագ զօրէղ:

　　　Գագեր.　　　հատանումն:

　　　Գալիլեա.　　հոլովական:

　　　Գադատացիք.　կաթեալք:

115	Behmovt',	sheep, or quadrupeds.
	Beniamin,	son of right hand.
	Benoni,	son of my affliction.
	Betul,	virgin.
	Bera,	well.
120	Bersabēē,	well of oath.
	Bet'dagon,	house of corn.
	Bēl,	aged.
	Bela,	swallower, or destroyer.
	Boyos,	in power.
125	Bosovr,	strength.
	Bresit',	The first book of the Law is named thus.
	Gabayea,	hill.
	Gabayad,	a casting./
303r	Gabriēl,	man God or of God.
130	Gat',	felicitous, or arriving quickly.
	Gadgad,	felicity of felicity, or quickly powerful.
	Gazer,	cutting.
	Galilea,	circular.
	Gałatac'ik',	those having dripped.

135	Գաղգաղայ.	անիւ կամ անդրադարձումն:
	Գեբադ.	սահման:
	Գեղէոն.	փշրող կամ կործանող:
	Գեհոն.	լանջիք.
	Գեհենին.	հովիտ տրամունքթեան:
140	Գերսմ.	պանդուխտ անդ:
	Գերսոն.	
	Գոզ.	տանիս:
	Գողգոթայ.	կառափելոյ տեղի այս է ուր
		գլուխք մեռելոց
		դնին:
	Գոդիաթ.	փոփոխ ... ումն
145	Գոմեր:	շափ:
	Գոմորայ.	ժողովուրդ ապտամբ:
	Դաբրէիովմին.	բանք աւուրց կամ գիրք:
	Դագոն.	ցորեան:
	Դալիլա.	աղքատութիւն:
150	Դաթան.	արարողութիւն կամ օրէնք:
303բ	Դամասկոս.	գող արեան կամ նմանութիւն բոցոյ
		կամ ծննդեան հոգար/կուբթիւն:
	Դան.	դատող կամ դատաստան:
	Դանիէլ.	դատաստան աստուծոյ:
	Դարեհ.	խնդրող:
155	Դալիթ.	սիրելի:
	Դեբովրա.	մեղուք կամ բան:

135	Gaɫgaɫay,	wheel, or retrogression.
	Gebaɫ,	limit.
	Gedēon,	crusher, or destroyer.
	Gehon,	lungs.
	Gehenin,	valley of sadness.
140	Gersom,	sojourner there.
	Gerson,	. . .
	Gog,	ceiling.
	Goɫgot'a,	place of execution, this is where the heads of the dead are placed.
145	Gomer,	measure.
	Gomoray,	people rebellion.
	Dabrēiovmin,	words of days, or a book.
	Dagon,	wheat.
	Dalila,	poverty.
150	Dat'an,	ceremony, or law.
303v	Damaskos,	dew of blood, or likeness of flame, or care of/birth.
	Dan,	judger, or judgement.
	Daniēl,	god's judgement.
	Dareh,	searcher.
155	Dawit',	beloved.
	Debovra,	bees, or word.

Դեկապոլիս.   ժ. քաղաքաց:

Դիաթրլոս.   ծործեալ:

Դիդիմոս.

160   Դիթալոսոն.   երկու ծովք:

Դինա.   դատաստան կամ դատող:

Դիոնիսիոս.   յաստուծոյ ցորեալ յունաց

                    է բառ:

Դովեկ.   տրամեալ կամ

                    աշխատեալ:

Դովր.   ծնունդ կամ լինելություն:

165   Դովրա.   ծնունդ կամ բնակություն:

Եբադ.   կոյտ հնութեան:

Եբեր.   ընկեր կամ հաղորդակից կամ

                    անցք:

Եբրայեցի.   անցաւոր:

Եզիպտոս.   նեղուածք կամ անձկություն:

170   Եզդոմ.   որթ:

Եղեմ.   վայելչություն կամ փափկություն:

Եղոմ.   կարմիր կամ երկրային:

Եզեկիա.   զորություն տեառն:

Եզեկիէլ.   զորություն աստուծոյ:

175   Եզրաս.   օգնական կամ զաւիթ:

Եզրիէլ.   օգնություն աստուծոյ:/

Dekapōlis,   of ten cities.

Diabolos,   having flowed

Didimos   . . .

160 Dit'alason,   two seas.

Dina,   judgement, or judger.

Dionisios,   bedewed by God; it is a

                          Greek word.

Dovek,   saddened, or having

                          laboured.

Dovr,   birth, or generation.

165 Dovra,   birth, or dwelling.

Eba⫠,   heap (or: meadow) of

                          antiquity.

Eber,   friend, or participating,

                          or passage.

Ebrayec'i,   one who passes.

Egiptos,   afflictions, or narrowness.

170 Eg⫠om,   calf.

Edem,   enjoyment, or delight.

Edom,   red, or earthly.

Ezekia,   lord' power.

Ezekiēl,   god's power.

175 Ezras,   helpful, or portico.

Ezriēl,   God's help./

304ա　　　　Եզրով.　　　　　նետ գնձութեան:

　　　　　Եթամ.　　　　　բաշունթիւն նոցա:

　　　　　Եթովպիա.　　　　յունարէն ջերմունթիւն եւ եբրայե-

　　　　　　　　　　　　ցերէն սեւունթիւն կամ սեաւ:

180　Եղզանայ.　　　　աստուած նախանձտ:

　　　Եղբանան.　　　　աստուծոյ շնորհք կամ ողորմունթիւն:

　　　Եղիա.　　　　　　աստուած տէր:

　　　Եղիակիմ.　　　　աստուծոյ յարունթիւն:

　　　Եղիազար.　　　　աստուծոյ օգնունթիւն:

185　Եղիմելէք.　　　　աստուած իմ արքայ:

　　　Եղինաթան.　　　　աստուած ետ:

　　　Եղիշէ.　　　　　　աստուծոյ փրկունթիւն կամ աստուած

　　　　　　　　　　　　　　　　　　　　　　　　փրկիչ:

　　　Եղիսաբեթ.　　　　աստուած երդման:

　　　Եկլեսիա <ս>տէս.　բարոզող:

190　Եմաւուս.　　　　երկիւղած ի խորհրդոյ:

　　　Եմմանուէլ.　　　ընդ մեզ աստուած:

　　　Ենգենիա.　　　　նաւակատիկ:

　　　Եննոն.　　　　　ա՞ա նմա:

　　　Ենովս.　　　　　մարդ կամ այր:

195　Ենովք.　　　　　ունխտեալ:

　　　Եսայիայ.　　　　փրկունթիւն տեառն:

　　　Եսաւ.　　　　　առնող կամ գործող:

　　　Եսթեր.　　　　　ծածկեալ:

　　　Ելբուլոս.　　　　ծարտար:

304r   Ezrov,   arrow of rejoicing.

          Et'am,   their bravery.

          Et'ovpia,   in Greek, warmth; and in Hebrew,

                           blackness or black.

180   Elkana,   jealous god.

          Elk'anan,   god's grace or mercy.

          Ełia,   god lord.

          Ełiakim,   rising of god.

          Ełiazar,   god's help.

185   Ełimelēk',   my god king.

          Ełinat'an,   god gave.

          Ełiše,   god's salvation or god saviour.

          Ełisabet',   god of oath.

          Eklesiastēs,preacher

190   Emawus,   fearing counsel.

          Emmanuēl,   god (is) with us.

          Enkenia,   inauguration.

          Ennon,   behold for him.

          Enovs,   human being, or man.

195   Enovk',   having promised.

          Esayia,   lord's salvation.

          Esaw,   doer, or maker.

          Est'er,   hidden.

          Eubulos,   ingenious.

200	Երամէել.	ողորմութիւն աստուծոյ:
	Երեմիա.	բարձրութիւն տեառն:
	Երիքով.	լուսին կամ ամիս:
	Երուսաղէմ.	տեսութիւն խաղաղութեան կամ տեսութիւն կատարեալ: /
304բ	Եւա.	կենդանի:
205	Եփրա<թայ>.	առատութիւն կամ պտղաբեր:
	Եփրայիմ.	պտղաբեր կամ աճող:
	Եփրոն.	հող կամ մոխիր:
	Զաբուղուն.	բնակութիւն:
	Զամրի.	երգող:
210	Զարայ.	արեւելք:
	Զաքարիայ.	յիշատակ տեառն:
	Զաքէոս.	անարատ:
	Զեբեդեա.	օժտեալ:
	Զեբէէ.	պատարագ:
215	Զորաբաբէլ.	օտար յամօթոյ
	Էլլեսմովթ.	երկրորդ գիրք օրինաց:
	Թադէոս.	բարեբանող:
	Թամար.	տերեւ կամ ոստ:
	Թարայ.	անուշահոտ:
220	Թարսիս.	խորհրդագածութիւն ուրախութեան:
	Թաւ.	նշան:
	Թափոր.	ընտրութիւն կամ մաքրութիւն:
	Թերաթիմ.	տիպք կամ կուռք:

200 Erameel,   god's mercy.

Eremia,   lord's exaltation.

Erik'ov,   moon or month.

Erusałem,   vision of peace, or perfect vision.

304v   Ewa,   living.

205 Ep'ra<t'a>, abundance, or fruitful.

Ep'rayim,   fruitful, or increasing.

Ep'ron,   dust, or ashes.

Zabulun,   dwelling.

Zamri,   singer.

210 Zaray,   east.

Zak'aria,   lord's memorial.

Zak'ēos,   immaculate.

Zebedea,   having given.

Zebee,   sacrifice.

215 Zorababel, strange to shame.

Ellesmovt', second book of the Law.

T'adēos,   praiser.

T'amar,   leaf or branch.

T'ara,   sweet-smelling.

220 T'arsis,   spiritual teaching of happiness.

T'aw,   sign.

T'ap'ōr,   election, or cleanliness.

T'erat'im, likeness, or idol.

	Թ <n> բէլ․	աշխարհի ստացուած։
225	Թովմաս․	անդունդք կամ խորք կամ կրկին։
	Թոփոթոր․	զանկակ կամ դարձուիթւն։
	ի <եզրաֈ>էլ․	զաւակ աստուծոյ։
	իթամար․	կղզի ոստոյ։
	իսահակ․	ծիծաղ։
230	իսաքար․	է վարձ կամ պարգեւ։
	իսմայէլ․	լուր աստուծոյ։/
305ա	իսրայէլ․	յաղթող աստուծոյ կամ տեսող
		աստուծոյ։
	Լիա․	աշխատեալ կամ վաստակեալ։
	Լիբանոս․	պայծառ։
235	Լիբիա․	եբրայեցերէն լուբիմ այս է սիրտ
	Լիթոստրոտոս․	քարամբք շարժեալ յունաց ծովու։
		է քար։
	Խառան․	աւերեալ․
	Կադէս․	սրբութիւն։
	Կահաթ․	ժողով։
240	Կային․	ստացուած կամ ստացեալ։
	Կանա․	նախանձ կամ հետեւումն։
	Կասթին	իբրեւ դեւք։
	Կարիաթարիմ․	քաղաք մայրեաց։
	Կարիաթսեփեր․	քաղաք նամակաց։
245	Կարկատ․	բլուր վկայութեան։
	Կարմէլ․	ծանուցումն Թլփտութեան կամ զառն
		Թլփատեալ։

T'ōbēl,   possession of world.

225   T'ovmas,   abyss, or depths, or double.

T'op'ot'or,   bell, or return.

I‹ezray›ēl,   god's seed.

It'amar,   branch's island.

Isahak,   laughter.

230   Isak'ar,   is reward, or offering.

Ismayēl,   god's listening. /

305r   Israyēl,   vanquisher of god, or seer of god.

Lia,   having toiled, or having laboured.

Libanos,   shining.

235   Libia,   Hebrew Lubim, that is heart of sea.

Lit'ostratos, moved by stones; it is a Greek

word.

Xaṙan,   destroyed.

Kadēs,   holiness.

Kahat',   gathering.

240   Kayin,   possession, or having possessed.

Kana,   envy or imitation.

Kast'in,   like demons.

Kariat'ari m, city of forests.

Kariat'sep'ēr, city of letters.

245   Karkaṫ,   hill of witness.

Karmel,   declaration of circumcision, or
               circumcised lamb.

	Կափանայում.	ազարակ ապաշխարութեան:
	Կեդար.	սեւութիւն կամ տրտմութիւն:
	Կեդրոն.	սեւեցեալ կամ տրտում:
250	Կերէաս.	ուրախ:
	Կեփաս.	պետրոս ի վիմէ:
	Կինովթ.	որթք:
	Կիս.	խոշոր:
	Կղէոպաս.	փառք աստուծոյ:
255	Կիպրոս.	գեղեցիկ:
	Կիւրոս.	իբրեւ թշուառական: /
305բ	Կողոսացիք.	պաղատանք ընծիg:
	Կորբան.	պարգեւ կամ ընծայ:
	Կորխա.	գոշող կամ կարդացող կամ կնդակ:
260	Հայաստան.	եբրայեցերէն արարադ որ է
		անէծք սասանութեան:
	Հերմոն.	աւերումն:
	Հելի.	ընծայ կամ պատարագ:
	Հելիպոդիս.	եբրայեցերէ ոն որ է
		վիշտ:
	Հնդատան	եբրայեցերէն սոփեր որ է
		քաղաքացի:
265	Հնդիկք.	գովութիւն:
	Հողէփեննէս.	քաշ գործգլուխ:
	Հորմ.	քարծր կամ վերամբարծ:

	Kap'aṙnayum,	village of penitence.
	Kedar,	blackness, or sadness.
	Kedron,	blackened, or sad.
250	Kerēas,	happy.
	Kep'as,	Petros, from rock.
	Kinovt',	lamentations.
	Kis,	rough.
	Kłeōpas,	glory of god.
255	Kipros,	beautiful.
	Kiwros,	as if miserable.
305v	Kołosac'ik',	supplications of prayers.
	Korban,	gift, or offering.
	Korxa,	caller, or reader, or bald.
260	Hayastan,	in Hebrew Ararat, which is curse of shaking.
	Hermon,	destruction.
	Heli,	offering, or sacrifice.
	Helipōlis,	in Hebrew On, which is affliction.
	Hndastan,	in Hebrew Sop'er, which is citizen.
265	Hndikk'	praise.
	Hołēp'eṙnēs,	brave general.
	Hṙom,	high, or exalted.

	Հռուβ.	լիացեալ:
	Ղաբան.	սպիտակ կամ պայծառ:
270	Ղազարոս.	աստուծոյ օգնութիւն:
	Ղամէք.	աղքատ կամ խոնարհեալ:
	Ղապիովբ.	փայլատակունք:
	Ղեկի.	որէնք:
	Ղելի.	շաղկապեալ:
275	Ղեքի.	կզակ:
	Ղելիաթան.	շաղկապ կամ ընկերութիւն իւր:
	Ղովա.	խառնեալ կամ պատեալ:
	Մայասիա.	գործ տեառն:
	Մաաքեա.	կողոպտեալ:
306ա 280	Մադիան./	դատաստան:
	Մաթուսաղայ.	զմահ իւր խնդրող:
	Մագդաղենացի.	մեծացեալ:
	Մակեդոն.	քաց:
	Մադաքիայ.	հրեշտակ տեառն:
285	Մադդէթ.	փառաբանող զաստուած
	Մադքոս.	թագաւոր:
	Մամզէք.	ի պոոնկէ ծրնեալ:
	Մամոնայ.	մեծութիւն կամ ստացուած:
	Մանայեմ.	մխիթարիչ:
290	Մանասէ.	մոոացումն:
	Մանովէ.	հանգիստ:

		Hłut',	**filled.**
		Łaban,	white, or brilliant.
	270	Łazaros,	god's help.
		Łamēk',	poor, or humbled.
		Łapiovt',	lightenings.
		Łeki,	law.
		Łewi,	joined.
	275	Łek'i,	chin.
		Łewiat'an,	junction, or his friendship.
		Łovt,	mixed, or surrounded.
		Mayasia,	lord's work.
		Maak'ea,	despoiled.
306r	280	Madian, /	judgement.
		Mat'usała,	seeker of his death.
		Magdałenac'i,	having increased.
		Makedon,	flame.
		Małak'ia,	lord's angel.
	285	Małałēt',	praiser of God.
		Małk'os,	king.
		Mamzēr,	born of a prostitute.
		Mamona,	greatness, or possession.
		Manayem,	comforter.
	290	Manasē,	forgetfulness.
		Manovē,	rest.

	Մառա.	*դառն.*
	Մասադոթ.	*գիրք առակաց*
		ասի:
	Մասեփա.	*պահապան:*
295	*Մասսա.*	*բեռն:*
	Մաթէոս.	*պարգեւեալ:*
	Մարթայ.	*կոչող:*
	Մարիամ.	*բարձրացեալ կամ դառնութեան*
		ծով:
	Մելքիա.	*թագաւոր տեառն:*
300	*Մելքիսեդէկ.*	*թագաւոր արդարութեան:*
	Մելքիսուայ.	*թագաւոր փրկիչ:*
	Մելքող.	*ով զամենայն:*
	Մեմփիբոստէ.	*ի բերանոյ ամօթոյ:*
	Մեսդամ.	*Խադադարար:*
305	*Մեսոպոտանիա.*	*միջագետ:*
	Միսափաթ,	*որ է կաղէս դատաստան:*
	Մեղբայ.	*արբայ:*
	Միբա.	*աղբատ:*
	Միբայէլ.	*ով իբրեւ զաստուած:*
310	*Միսիա.*	*զազիր: /*
306բ	*Միքիա.*	*ով իբրեւ զտէր:*
	Միսայէլ.	*ով խնդրուածք:*
	Մնէս.	*լիար քանքար տես յեզէ. լբ.:*

	Mara,	bitter.
	Masałot',	the Book of Proverbs is said (thus).
	Masep't,	guardian.
295	Massa,	burden.
	Mat'ēos,	presented.
	Mart'a,	caller.
	Mariam,	elevated, or sea of bitter-ness.
	Melk'ia,	lord's king.
300	Melk'isedek,	king of justice.
	Melk'isua,	king saviour.
	Melk'oł.	who all.
	Memp'ibost'ē,	from shame's mouth.
	Mesołam,	peacemaker.
305	Mesopotania,	between river(s).
	Misp'at',	which is Kadēs, judgement.
	Mełk'a,	king.
	Mik'a,	poor.
	Mik'ayēl,	who is like god?
310	Misia,	ugly./
306v	Mik'ia,	who is like the lord?
	Misayēl,	who? question.
	Mnēs,	litre, talent, see Ezek. 38.

Մովաբ.	ի հօրէ:
315 Մովսա.	քառըն կամ բենն:
Մովսէս.	ի ջրոյ հանեալ:
Մոգ.	իմաստասէր կամ փիլ֊ սոփոս:
Յակոբ.	խաբող:
Յամին.	աջ:
320 Յայէլ.	համբարձումն կամ վայրի այծ:
Յայիէլ.	կենդանի է աստուած:
Յասն.	բժշկող:
Յաբէթ.	լայնացեալ:
Յեբուս.	երուսադէմ կամ աբացումն:
325 Յերապոլիս.	սուրբ քաղաք:
Յեբրւսթէ.	այր ամօթոյ:
Յեմենի.	աջ:
Յէու.	ինքնինէն:
Յէուս.	խրատող կամ ցեզ:
330 Յեսբոք.	է ունայն:
Յեսսէ.	էութիւն կամ էակ կամ պարգեւ:
Յեսու.	տէր փրկիչ:
Յերորադ.	մարանշող ընդ կոոց:
Յերորովամ.	մարանշող ընդ ժողովրդեան:

Movab,	from father.
315 Movsa,	unleavened bread, or burden.
Movsēs,	drawn forth from water.
Mog,	lover of wisdom, or philosopher.
Yakob,	deceiver.
Yamin,	right hand.
320 Yayēl,	elevation, or goat of field.
Yayiēl,	god is living.
Yason,	healer.
Yabet',	having broadened.
Yebus,	Jerusalem, or kicking.
325 Yerapōlis,	sacred city.
Yebust'ē,	man of shame.
Yemeni,	right hand.
Yēu,	from self.
Yēus,	advisor, or moth.
330 Yespōk',	it is empty.
Yessē,	existence, or being, or offering.
Yesu,	lord, redeemer.
Yeroboał,	fighter with idol.
Yerobovam,	fighter with people.

335 Յեփթայէ .   բացող:

Յիսուս .   տէր փրկիչ եբրայեցերէն

                       յէուսուլայ:

Յոթորայ .   վեհագոյն: /

307ա Յեքոնիա .   պատրաստութիւն տեառն:

Յոբ .   վշտագին կամ ողբացող:

340 Յուդայ .   գովութիւն:

Յուլիոս .   բրատա:

Յուննան .   աղաւնի:

Յովաք .   հայրութիւն կամ ունոդ հայր:

Յովակիմ .   տեառն յարութիւն:

345 Յովաս .   տեառն հուր կամ անմիաբան

                       կամ յուսահատեալ կամ ցեց:

Յովաքիմ .   տեառն պատրաստութիւն:

Յովէլ .   կամեցող կամ սկսանող:

Յովհաննէս .   շնորհալի կամ արդար կամ

                       ողորմած:

Յովնադաբ .   կամաւոր:

350 Յովնա ⟨թ⟩ան .   տեառն պարգեւ:

Յովնան .   արդար կամ ողորմած:

Յովսափատ .   տէր դատաւոր:

Յովսէփ .   տեառն աճումն:

Յովսիա .   հուր տեառն:

335   Yep't'ayē,   opener.

       Yisus,   lord, saviour, in Hebrew

                  Yḛusuay

       Yot'ora,   supreme./

307r   Yek'onia,   lord's **pre**paration.

       Yob,   grievous, or lamenter.

340   Yuda,   praise.

       Yulios,   earthen (?).

       Yunan,   dove.

       Yovab,   paternity, or having a father.

       Yovakim,   lord's rising.

345   Yovas,   lord's fire, or disagreeing,

                    or having despaired, or moth.

       Yovak'im,   lord's preparation.

       Yovēl,   desirer, or beginner.

       Yovhannēs,   gracious, or just, or merci-

                    ful.

       Yovnadab,   willing.

350   Yovnat'an,   lord's offering.

       Yovnan,   just, or merciful.

       Yovsap'at.   lord judge.

       Yovsēp',   lord's increase.

       Yovsia,   lord's fire.

355 Յեղովմէ．　　　　　կարմիր կամ երկրային։

Յեգունիա．　　　　　հազագանդութիւն տեառն։

Յովրամ．　　　　　բարձր կամ վեհագոյն։

Յորդանան．　　　　　զետ դատաստանի։

Յոքաս．　　　　　տեառն ըմբռնումն կամ ըմբռնող։

360 Յոյնք．　　　　　եբրայեցերէն յելայիմ այս է

խաբեբայք։

Նայասն．　　　　　օձ։

Նաբաթ．　　　　　կամաւոր։

Նաբաղ．　　　　　անմիտ։

307բ　　Նաբովթ．　　　　　խորք／կամ մարգարէութիւն։

365 Նաբուզզողոննոսոր． սուգ դատասանի։

Նազարեթ．　　　　　սրբեալ կամ բաժանեալ կամ

պահպանեալ կամ ծաղկեալ։

Նազովրացիք．　　　　　բաժանեալք կամ սրբաալք։

Նաթան．　　　　　բաշխեալ կամ պարգեւեալ։

Նաթանայէլ．　　　　　պարգեւ աստուծոյ։

370 Նային．　　　　　գեղեցիկ։

Նաւում．　　　　　մխիթարիչ։

Նաբովր．　　　　　շորացեալ։

Նէեման．　　　　　գեղեցիկ։

Նէապոլիս．　　　　　նոր քաղաք։

355	Yedovmē,	red, or earthy.
	Yezonia,	lord's obedience.
	Yovram,	high or supreme.
	Yordanan,	river of judgement.
	Yok'az,	lord' seizing or seizer.
360	Yoynk',	in Hebrew Yewayim, that is deceivers.
	Nayason,	serpent.
	Nabat',	willing.
	Nabaɫ,	foolish.
307v	Nabovt',	pit,/or prophecy.
365	Nabugodonosor,	mourning of judgement.
	Nazaret',	sanctified, or separated, or guarded, or having flowered.
	Nazorac'ik',	separated ones, or sanctified ones.
	Nat'an,	distributed, or offered.
	Nat'anayēl,	god's offering.
370	Nayin,	beautiful.
	Naum,	comforter,
	Nak'ovr,	dried up.
	Nēeman,	beautiful.
	Nēapōlis,	new city.

375　Նեբրովթ.　　　ապստամբ:

　　Նէեմի.　　　մխիթարութիւն:

　　Նէովստան.　　պղնձի:

　　Նեփթայիմ.　　գուզաւորութիւն:

　　Նինուէ.　　　գեղեցիկ:

380　Նոյ.　　　　　դադարումն կամ հանգիստ:

　　Նոյոմին.　　　զարդարեալ կամ գեղեցիկ:

　　Նուարեղղաբր.　գիրք թըւոց:

　　Շաբթ.　　　　հանգիստ կամ դադարումն:

　　Շուշանայ.　　վարդ կամ շուշան:)

385　Ալդոդմ.　　　վկայութեն նոցա:

　　Անէսիմէոս.　　օգտակար:

　　Օզա.　　　　զօրութիւն:

　　Օզիա.　　　զօրութիւն տեառն:

　　Օզիէլ.　　　զօրութիւն աստուծոյ:/

308ա　390　Օղա.　　　վրաա կամ խորան:

　　Ոռնամ.　　　վիշտ:

　　Օվբաթիայ.　　ծառայ տեառն:

　　Օվբէթ.　　　ծառայ:

　　Օվբ.　　　　քաղարծ:

395　Օվնանայ.　　վիշտ կամ անիրաւութիւն

　　Օվսէէ.　　　փրկիչ:

　　Օվրէփ.　　　ազաւ:

　　Որդի եկրայ.　　գիրք դեւտական:

375	Nebrovt',	rebellion.
	Nēemi,	consolation.
	Nēovstan,	of bronze.
	Nep't'ayim,	equality.
	Ninuē,	beautiful.
380	Noy,	cessation, or rest.
	Noyomin,	decorated, or beautiful.
	Nuareddabr,	Book of Numbers.
	Šabat',	rest, or cessation.
	Šušanay,	rose, or lily.
385	Odołom,	their witness.
	Onēsimēos,	helpful.
	Oza,	might.
	Ozia,	lord's might.
	Oziēl,	god's might. /
308r 390	Oła,	tent, or pavilion.
	Ornam,	affliction.
	Ovbat'ia,	lord's servant.
	Ovbēt',	servant.
	Ovk',	unleavened bread.
395	Ovnanay,	suffering, or injustice.
	Ovsēē,	saviour.
	Ovrēp',	raven.
	Ordi ekra,	Book of Leviticus.

Ուրիայ.　　　　　　　Յուր տեառն:

400 Որգիայ.　　　　　　ընբրնունմն:

Պադիստինէ.　　　　　մոխրով արկեալ:

Պարակեւէ.　　　　　պատրաստութիւն:

Պասեք.　　　　　　　անցք:

Պենտէկոստ.　　　　　յիսներորդ:

405 Պետրոս.　　　　　վէմ:

Ջերոնիմոս.　　　　սուրբ անուն:

Ռաբաթ.　　　　　　յոլով կամ մեծ:

Ռագուէլ.　　　　　Յովիւ աստուծոյ:
410 Ռահաք.　　　　　ամբարտաւան կամ քաշ:
Ռախաբ.　　　　　լայնացեալ:

Ռամայ.　　　　　վերամբարձ:

Ռամեսէ.　　　　որոտումն ցեցոյ:

Ռափայէլ.　　　　բժշկութիւն կամ դեղ աստուծոյ:

Ռափայիմ.　　　　Յակայք կամ բժիշկք:

415 Ռաքէլ.　　　　ոչխար:

Ռեմոն.　　　　　նոնենի: /
308բ Ռեսփայ.　　　　սատկութիւն:

Ռեբեկայ.　　　　կուշտ:

Ռեքաբ.　　　　　կառք:

420 Ռուբէն.　　　　տեսանող զորդի:

Ռորովամ.　　　բազմացուցանող զժողովուրդ:

Սաբայ.　　　　　դարձումն կամ գերութիւն կամ
　　　　　　　　　շրջագայութիւն:

Սաբաովթ.　　　　զօրք:

	Uria,	lord's fire.
400	Ok'ozia,	seizure.
	Pałistinē,	cast of ashes.
	Paraskewē,	preparation.
	Pasek',	passing.
	Pentēkost,	fiftieth.
405	Petros,	rock.
	J̆eronimos,	holy name.
	Ṙabat',	great, or large.
	Ṙaguēl,	god's shepherd.
410	Ṙahab,	proud, or brave.
	Ṙaxab,	broadened.
	Ṙama,	elevated.
	Ṙamesē,	thunder of moth.
	Ṙap'ayēl,	healing or medicine of god.
	Ṙap'ayim	giants or doctors.
415	Ṙak'ēl,	sheep.
	Ṙemon,	pomegranate-tree./
	Ṙesp'a,	violence.
	Ṙebeka,	side.
	Ṙek'ab,	chariot.
420	Ṙubēn,	seeing the son.
	Robovam,	increasing the people.
	Saba,	return, or captivity, or going around.
	Sabaovt',	armies.

308v

		Սաղուկեցիք	*արդարք:*
425		*Սաղա.*	*առաքումն:*
		Սաղիմ.	*խաղաղութիւն:*
		Սաղմանասար.	*խաղաղութիւն հաստատեալ:*
		Սաղմոն.	*խաղաղարար:*
		Սաղպաղ.	*հովանի երկիւղի:*
430		*Սամարիա.*	*պահապանութիւն:*
		Սամփսոն.	*արեգակն նորա կամ անուան*
			կրկնութիւն:
		Սամուէլ.	*ընդել յաստուծոյ:*
		Սառայ.	*տիրուհի կամ անեւշահոտ:*
		Սատանայ.	*ոսոխ կամ փոխ առեալ:*
435		*Սառայի.*	*տիրուհի իմ:*
		Սարոնայ.	*մակրդակ:*
		Սաւուղ.	*խնդրեալ կամ արուես:*
		Սափատ.	*դատող:*
		Սեղեկիա.	*արդար տեառն:*
440		*Սեղիմ.*	*տարածումն:*
		Սէթ.	*եղեալ:*
		Սեգովր.	*փոքր:*
		Սելում.	*խաղաղարար կամ մնացող:*
		Սեհոն.	*արմատախիլ:/*
309ա	445	*Սեղովմ.*	*յատակող:*
		Սեմ.	*անուն կամ համբաւ կամ եղեալ:*

		Sadukec'ik',	just ones.
	425	Saɬa,	sending.
		Saɬim,	peace.
		Saɬmanasar,	established peace.
		Saɬmon,	peace-maker.
		Saɬpaad,	shadow of fear.
	430	Samaria,	guarding.
		Samp'son,	his sun, or repetition of name.
		Samuēl,	accustomed by god.
		Saṙa,	mistress, or sweet-smelling.
		Satana,	adversary, or having borrowed.
	435	Sarayi,	my mistress.
		Sarona,	⌈ one word ⌉
		Sawuɬ,	having asked, or fox.
		Sap'at,	judge.
		Sedēkia,	lord's just one.
	440	Sedim,	extension.
		Sēt',	placed.
		Segor,	small.
		Selum,	peace-maker, or remaining.
		Sehon,	rooted out./
309r	445	Seɬovm,	destroyer.
		Sem,	name, or fame, or placed.

Սեմէի.	ꞈնազանդ կամ ա̈նուն իմ:
Սենեքերիմ.	մորենի աւերման:
Սէոն.	ꞈնչումն:
450 Սեպովրայ.	գեղեցիկ կամ փող կամ թռչուն կամ ̄ծրնⴼդուկ:
Սելովամ.	առաքեալ կամ առաքող:
Սիբայ.	զօրք:
Սիբողդէթ.	բեռն:
Սիմէովն.	լսող կամ լուր:
455 Սիմօն.	ꞈնազանդ:
Սին.	մորենի կամ զէն կամ վաꞈան:
Սիոն.	կոյտ:
Սիսարայ.	գⴼիⴼծառն տեսանող:
Սիլքեմ.	բազուկ:
460 Սէքոր.	սեաւ կամ խառնեալ կամ նեղոս:
Սկարիովտացի.	այր սպանութեան:
Սոդոմ.	խորꞈուրդ նոցա:
Սոմեր.	պաꞈապան:
Սովմացի.	ննⴼ ⴼող:
465 Սորեկ.	այգի:
Սոփիդիմ.	դատաւորք.
Ստեփաննոս.	պսակեալ:
Վաքաբովդ.	ուր փառք կամ վայ փառաց:
Տարսս.	թեւաւոր:

Semei,	obedient, or my name.
Senēk'ērim,	thorn-bush of destruction.
Sēon,	noise.
450 Sep'ovra,	beautiful, or trumpet, or bird,
	or sparrow.
Selovam,	sent, or sender.
Siba,	army.
Sibołet',	burden.
Simēon,	hearer, or hearing.
455 Simōn,	obedient.
Sin,	thorn-bush, or weapon, or shield.
Sion,	heap.
Sisara,	seeing the sparrow.
Siwk'em,	arm.
460 Sik'or	black, or mixed, or Nile.
Skariovtac'i,	man of killing.
Sodom,	their secret.
Somēr,	guard.
Sovmnac'i,	sleeper.
465 Sorek,	vineyard.
Sop'idim,	judges.
Step'annos,	crowned.
Vak'abovd,	where glory, or woe of glory.
Tarsos,	winged.

470 Տիմէոս.   կոյր կամ կուրութիւն:

Տիմոթէոս.   պատիւ աստուծոյ յունաց է բառ: /

309բ   Տիտոս.   պատուական:

Տիւրացիք.   նեղացեալք:

Տուբիայ.   բարի տէր:

475 Փակէէ.   բացող:

Փանուէլ.   տեսանող զաստուած:

Փասկա.   թլուր:

Փարաւոն.   ցրուող:

Փարէգ.   բաժանումն կամ ձիաւոր:

480 Փարիսեցիք.   բաժանեալք:

Փենէֆէգ.   երես հալատոյ:

Փոքոր.   վիհ:

Փութ.   ապրիկայ:

Փաղեկ.   բաժանումն:

485 Քաղդեաստան.   եբրայեցերէն կազդին այս է իբրեւ դեւք:

Քազբի.   ստախոսք:

Քաղէք.   իբրեւ զմիրա:

Քամ.   ջերմ կամ ջերմութիւն:

Քանան.   վաճառական:

490 Քեբրոն.   բարեկամութիւն կամ ընկերութիւն:

Քետուրա.   անուշահոտ:

470 Timēos,   blind, or blindness.

    Timot'ēos,   god's honour, it is a Greek
                   word./

309v   Titos,   honourable.

        Tiwrac'ik',   afflicted ones.

        Tubiay,   good lord.

475 P'akēē,   opener.
    P'anuēl,   seeing God.

    P'aska,   hill.

    P'arawon,   scatterer.

    P'arez,   division, or equestrian.

480 P'arisec'ik,   divided ones.

    P'enēnēz,   face of faith.

    P'ok'or,   gulf.

    P'ut',   Africa.

    P'aɫek,   division.

485 K'aɫdeastan,   Hebrew Kazdin, that is: like
                   demons.

    K'azbi,   speaker of lies.

    K'aɫeb,   like the heart.

    K'am,   hot or heat.

    K'anan,   merchant.

490 K'ebron,   friendship or company.

    K'etura,   sweet-smelling.

Քոր.   լեառն:

Քորեբ.   անապատ:

Քորազին.   խորհուրդ:

495 Քուշ.   եթովբացի:

Քուս.   խրատ:

Քրիստոս.   օծեալ:

K'or,   mountain.

K'oreb,   desert.

K'orazin, secret.

495 K'uš,   Ethiopian.

K'us,   counsel.

K'ristos, anointed.

1   յեբրայեցոց 55 81   2   հայր} 88   om 55 |

3   անցանօք 55   4 աբահւ 55   8 աբեթնագով 55

10 յունայնութիւն 55   11 աբբենէր 55   14 աբի-

այթար 55   16 աբիմէլէք} 55   աբդիմելէք 81

17 աբինաթաբ 55   19 om 55   21   աբրամմ } 55

աբրամ 81   23   ազաբ} 55   ազահ 81   26   պանտուխդ

55   27 յերկնային 55 | կարմի 81   28 ադռնայ

55   29 ադռնայի} 55   ադռնիա 81   30 ադռնիայ.

տիրող 55   31 ազարիայ 55   32 կողուպուտ 55

34 աթադիայ 55   38 ալէլուիա 81 | օրՀնեցէք 55

39 ալէքսանդէր 81 | քաՀ 55   40 ադքսանդրիա 55|

եբրա 55 81 | նոյ} 81 om 55 | Հումմ} 55   Հրոսմ

81   41 ամադէկ 55   44 ամանա 55   46 տէրու-

թիւն 55   47 ամեսայի քաՀ 55   48 ամեսայի} 55

ամէսիա 81   49 Հատատ 55   51 ամռն 55

53   քաՀ Հայրն եսայեա + մարգարէին erased 55 | է } 81

om   55   54 մարգարէն է} 55 om 81   56   աննանիայ

55   58   ուրախար 55   61 անտիոքայ 55   62

ապօդոս 55   68 ասքայ 55   74 արիթակոս 55

արիսպագոս 88   76 արտաքսերքէս 55   արտաքսերսէս 81

| ծառայգայթ 55 | անէծ 81   77 արբագասթ 81

78 եղբայր 55 | Հօր} 55   տեառն 81   79 աբիմէլէք

55 80 աքայիայ 55   82 աբիտոքէլ 55   ակիտոփէլ 81

84 բաթուէ որդիութիւն 55   86 after ln 88   55 |

ռաքէլայ 55 | ծեռացեալ կամ զարՀուրեալ } 55 om 81

87 totum om 81   89 քալլայ 55   91   քանեռգէս

55   92   քատո 55   94 քարիովնայ 55   98 քար-

տէմէոս 55   99 քէեդ զեքիւդ 55   101 քեթանիայ

55   103 քեդթաւան 81   104 քէթէլ 55   105

քէթէր 55   106 քեդդաՀէմ 81   107 դուսար} տուն

55   108 քեդասքէէ 81   109 քեդասմիուս 81

110 քեդասյիդայ 81   111 քեդբագէ 81   112 քեդ-

քագովր 81 | անդրնդոց 55   114 քելքեգովր 81

115 քէՀմովթ 81   121 քեթագռն 55 | ցորեննյ 55

123 քե[այ 55   126 քէրէսիթ 55   127 զապայա 55

128 զաքայաթ 55   131 զաթզաթ 55   զօրեդ } զօրբ

55   137 զէթոն 55   143 գլուխ 81* գլուխք 81°
| դնի 81   144 գողիաղ 81   145 գլմոր 55
146 գոմորա 55   149 դալիա 55   150 դաղան 55
151 բոգո 81   153 ասուածոյ } om 55   158 դիա-
պոլոս 81   159 դիդիմնոս 55   162 դէոնէսիոս 81
166 ինութեան} 55 ինազանդութեան 81   170 եզլով
55   173 եզէկիայ 55   174 եզէկիէլ 55   178
բաշութիւն 55   179 եթովփիայ 55 | յունարէն} 81
om 55   ատվութիւն 55   180 ելզանա 55   181
ելեքանան 55   182 եղիայ 55   185 եղիմէլէք 55 |
իմ } 81 om 55   189 եկլեսիաստէս 55 եկլիսիաստէկես
81   192 նաւակատիք 55   196 եսայիա 55   199
om 81   200 երամմէլ 55   204 կենդա 55   205
երրաթայ 55 եփրայ 81   206 երրայիմ 55   208
զաքոն 55   210 զարա 55   213 զեբեթեա 55
215 ամոթոյ 55   216 զլլեամվղ 55   217 Թաթէոս
55   219 Թարա 55   222 Թաբոր 81   224
< Թոբէլ >} Թովէլ 55 Թոբէլ 81   225 Թով 55
230 իսքար 55   232 իէլ . 81   233 լհայ 55
235 լիբիայ 55   236 բարամբ շարեալ 55   238
խաթէս 55   243 կարիթարիմ 55   244 կարիաթէփեր
55   251 կեփաս} illeg sign follows   55   252
կինովղ 55   254 կէլէոպաս 55   259 կամ 2°} om
55 ինայեասատան 81   262 ընձա 55   263 ինելի-
պոլիս 55   266 բաշ 55 | զորեղ 55*   271
լամեք 55 | խնարինել 55   273 դեղելի 55   275
դեք 55   279 մպաքեա 55   285 մաղադէթ 55
287 ծնեալ 55   293 մասաղովլթ 55   294 մասեփայ
55   297 մարթա 55   299 մելքիայ 55 | տէր 55
300 մելքիսեթեկ 55   304 մեսոպոտանիայ 55   307
om 55   308 om 81   314 մովփի 55   315
մովաս 81   317 փիլոսոփայ 55*   320 ինամբարծեալ
55 327 յեմէնի 55   329 յենւ 55   333 մարանոդ
81   335 յեբթայէ 55   339 ողբացող} 55 ապեցող
81   341 բրդոտ 55   343 յովփի 55   349-351
om 81   350 յովնաթան } յովնադան 55

352 յովսափաթ *55* *354* յովսիայ *55* *355* յեթովմէ
55 *357* վեհագոյն *55* *359* յոբազ *55* *365*
նանբոգոթոնոսոր *55* *368* նանթան *55* | բաշխեալ
81 պարգեւել *55* *369* աստուծոյ } + նային պարգեւ
աստուծոյ *55* *373* նէման *55* *375* ներրովդ *55*
376 նէմի *55* *377* նէոստան պղրնձի *55* *378*
նեփայիմ *55* *382* նուարեղղաբեր գիրգ *55* *383*
նաբաթ *55* *384* շուշաննայ *55* *387* ոգա } *55*
ուլա *81* գօրուԹիւն---գօրուԹիւն (ln *388*)} om *55*:
hmt *392* ողբադիայ *81* *395* ովնաննա *55* *397*
ովէփ ռազաւ *81* *398* դեւտական գիրբ *55* *399*
ուրիա *55* *400* որոգիա *55* *401* պադեսդինէ *55* |
մովրով *81* *404* պենտակոստ *55* *406* ջերոնիմոս
55 *408* հովիվ *55* *410* բաշ *55* *413*
ոպփայէլ *55* *414* ռայփայիմ բմիշբ *55* *416* ռեմմոն *55*
417 ռեփա *55* *418* ռեբեկա *55* *419* om *81*
420 ռորէն *55* *421* գձողովուրդն *55* *422* սառա
55 *423* սափավլովթ *55* *425* *81* *426*
սադէմ *55* *429* սադպատթ *55* *430* սամբսոն *81* |
արեգակ *81* | կրթուԹիւն *81* *432* րնդել} *81* եղեալ
55 *433* սառա *55* *434* սատանա *55* *435*
սարոնա *55* *436* աղուէստ *55* *438* սափաթ *55*
441 սէդ *81* *442* սեգոբրով *55* *443* սելլում *55*
444 սեհէն արմատահիլ *81* *447* սիմէի *55* *448*
սենեբիմ *55* *449* սեոն *55* *450* սեփովրա *55*
452 սիբա *55* *453* սիբողեդ *81* *457* սիննոյն *55*
458 սիսարա գձիծռան *55* *461* սպաննուԹեան *55*
463 սեմեբ *81* *464* սոմնացի *55* *465* յայզի *55*
468 վայբայբովդ *55* *470* կոբուԹին *55* *477*
փասբայ *81* *478* ցրւոդ *81* *479* փարէս *55*
480 փարեսեցիբ *55* *484* փադեբ *55* *485* բադ-
դէասման *55* կասԹին *55* *486* սաբխոդ *81* *487*
բադէփ *55* *490* բեփրոն *55* բարեկամուԹին} *81*
բարեբանուԹին *55* *493* բորէփ *55*

ln 2   Ona III ln 2.

ln 3   Ona III ln 1.

ln 4   Contrast Ona III ln 5, Ona I ln 6A, "Abdiu,
              promised servant". Compare the text of Wutz'
              Greek group V 1   Ἀβδΐοῦ, δουλεῦων κυρΐῳ
              (p. 705), Coisl, 10 (p. 714), Ona II ln 5
              Աբդիու. ծառայելով :   "Abdiu, by serving".

ln 5   Ona III ln 4.

ln 6   Ona III ln 6.

ln 7   Not in Ona II, III. Is comparable, but not
              identical with Ona I ln 57, cf. variae lectio-
              nes there.

ln 8   Ona III ln 3.

ln 9   Abel appears as "mourning" in Ona I, II. No
              exact parallel to the text here appears in any
              of Wutz' lists.

ln 10   Ona III ln 8.

ln 11   Compare Ona I, ln 51 "father or son of candle".

ln 12   Ona III ln 18.

ln 13   Ona III ln 10.

ln 14   Ona III ln 11 is similar but not identical: cf.
              Ona I ln 43.

ln 15   This etymology for "Abigayil", Ona III ln 14.
              See Wutz p. 483 on variation of form.

ln 16   Ona III ln 16. The reading of 81 "Abdimelēk"
              is corrupt.

ln 17   Cf. Ona III ln 19. Wutz (p. 100**2**) points out
         that the etymologies of "Nadab" names in Ona III
         show an original <u>sponsalis</u> instead of the cor-
         rect <u>spontalis</u> or <u>spontanaeus</u>, suggesting an
         origin of at least some of the etymologies of
         Ona III in a Latin onomasticon. Note, however,
         that this present list reads "willing". It also
         differs in its translation from Ona I ln 15.

ln 18   No parallels to this name and etymology are
         evident in Wutz' materials.

ln 19   Ona III ln 17:55 omits completely.

ln 20   Ona III ln 21.

ln 21   Ona III ln 23: the form "Abra(h)am" is correct,
         cf. MS 55. The confusion of "Abraham" and
         "Abram" is common in the onomastica.

ln 22   Ona III ln 22.

ln 23   Compare Ona III, ln 24: the form of the name
         there is <u>Agabos</u>, which also occurs at Ona I with
         a different etymology. "Locust" occurs only
         here and in Ona III, deriving from Hebrew
         חגב; cf. Wutz, p. 963, n. 24.

ln 24   The etymology for "Agag" in Ona III ln 25 uses
         a different word for "roof" and is combined with
         that for "Agal". See also Wutz, pp. 483f.

ln 25   Ona III, ln 37.

ln 26   Ona III, ln 26, Ona II ln 56.

ln 27   In Ona III ln 28 the wording is different. Wutz
         has *երկաւոր* "twin" for *երկրաւոր* "earthly", pre-
         sumably printer's error. In MS 55 *յերկնաւոր*
         "heavenly" is found, a not uncommon confussion,
         see Arm IV Ezra 6:20 D.

ln 28   Ona III ln 29.

ln 29   Ona III ln 30: the form found in MS 55 is preferable to the "Adona" of MS 81, see next ln.
Wutz, note ad loc sees a mistranslation from
Latin in Ona III which read domini mei as a
genitive singular instead of a nominative plural. The plural is presented here.

ln 30   Ona III ln 31.

ln 31   Ona III ln 32.

ln 32   Ona III ln 34, Ona II ln 17.

ln 33   "Azotos", i.e. Ashdod; Ona II, ln 17, Ona III,
ln 33.

ln 34   Ona III ln 35.

ln 35   Ona III ln 38.

ln 36   Ona III ln 39.

ln 37   Ona III ln 40.

ln 38   Cf. Ona III ln 41, Ona I ln 56. The forms in
MS 55 for lns 38-9 with η "$\pm$" have been preferred, as the alphabetical order requires.
These are also the more ancient. In ln 40,
too, MS 55 has been followed for consistency's
sake.

ln 39   See Ona III ln 42 and Wutz, note in loc.

ln 40   Ona III ln 43. ꜱnₗⅆ "cruel" or "raw" is the
reading there as in MS 55. In MS 81 there is
a corrupt reading ꜱₗnnⅆ "Rome".

ln 41   Unlike Ona III ln 44, Ona I ln 29. Equivalent
to Ona III ln 51, "Amełik, king".

ln 42   Ona III ln 45.

ln 43   Ona III ln 47 for similar etymology but different wording.

ln 44   Ona III ln 46.

ln 45   i.e. Habakkuk; no parallel to this etymology is to be found among Wutz' texts.

ln 46   Cf. Ona III lns 60-61. This entry disturbs the alphabetical order.

ln 47   Cf. Ona III ln 48; but there the wording differs. The name there is "Amasayi", cf. ln 55 "Amesayi", here. See ln 48.

ln 48   Cf. Ona III ln 49: but there the wording differs. The form of name in MS 55 has been preferred to "Amesia" of MS 81. It resembles Ona III ln 49, fits the alphabetical order, and provides a basis for the etymology עם + שי .

ln 49   Ona III ln 52.

ln 50   Cf. Ona III ln 53 and commentary on ln 17, supra.

ln 51   Ona III ln 54.

ln 52   Ona III ln 55: but there "Amnon".

ln 53   Cf. Ona III ln 57.

ln 54   Cf. Ona III ln 58: the words "it is the prophet" found only in MS 55, seem on the basis of Ona III to be original.

ln 55   i.e. "the Amorite"; Ona III ln 56.

ln 56   Ona III, ln 62.

ln 57   Cf. Ona I ln 33: there the words "or song" are not found.

ln 58 Cf. Ona I ln 80 "Angē, feasts" which is found
in Greek (Wutz, pp. 694, 740) and Syriac
(Wutz, pp. 793, 829, et.al.).

ln 59 Cf. Ona III ln 63: different wording.

ln 60 This exact interpretation does not occur else-
where. For another based on χάρις etc. see
Ona III ln 64 and for discussion of the stem in
Onomastica, see Wutz, pp. 106 ff.

ln 61 Ona III ln 65: wording differs.

ln 62 No Armenian parallels. For the type of reading
serving as a source for this, see Wutz, p. 457,
deriving from stem פלא"א and perhaps, by trans-
position, א"לפ . A Greek Ἀπολλῶς also exists,
ibid.

ln 63 Cf. Ona III ln 69.

ln 64 See Esther 1:9 etc., Greek ἀστιν . No parallels
exist in Wutz' lists.

ln 65 Ona III ln 71 : there is no parallel to վերա-
նող "ascender, one who ascends".

ln 66 Ona III ln 70.

ln 67 Ona III ln 72: wording differs.

ln 68 Cf. Ona III ln 93: the name there is "Ak'sa".

ln 69 i.e. Arabians; see Ona III 94: the word երե-
կական generally means "belonging to yesterday".
This must be an inner-Armenian confusion for
"of the evening", as is indicated by Ona III
ibid.

ln 70 i.e. Arabians, Ona III ln 75: wording differs.

ln 71   Ona III ln 76.

ln 72   Ona III lns 77-78

ln 73   See Ona I, variant reading, Wutz p. 866 n., cf.
           Ona III ln 79.

ln 74   Ona III ln 82: the text of 81 contains a gra-
           phic corruption *n* o̲ > *u* s̲, producing the reading
           "Arispagos". The correction is supported by
           Ona III ibid.

ln 75   Ona I, Wutz p. 852 n. to ln 22.

ln 76   Ona III ln 86: the text is restored on the
           basis of the readings of MSS 55 and 81.

ln 77   Ona III ln 87.

ln 78   Ona III ln 88: MS 81 reads եղբայր աեաոն
           "lord's brother" which appears corrupt.

ln 79   Ona III ln 91: MS 55 reads Աբիմելէք "Abimelēk"
           which appears corrupt.

ln 80   Cf. Ona III ln 89: the wording differs.

ln 81   Ona III ln 90.

ln 82   Ona III ln 92.

ln 83   Cf. Ona III ln 97: "shame" arises from a dif-
           ferent interpretation of the idea of confusion.

ln 84   Ona I ln 132 reads, as would be expected,
           "daughter of God". MS 55 "Bat'uē, sonship of
           God" is no more explicable than the text of MS
           81 is given here.

ln 85   Ona III ln 94: difference in wording.

ln 86   Cf. Ona I ln 133 and Wutz, pp. 281-2 for meaning "aged". No parallel for "amazed" (an etymology doubtless derived from Hebrew בהל) seems
to occur in Wutz. MS 55 is somewhat fuller than
MS 81 at this point and has some variation in
the order of names; see apparatus. This and
the following names commencing with "B" are not
included in Ona III.

ln 87   No parallels to this etymology of the name occur in Wutz' materials. For its basis, see the
preceding note.

ln 88   The etymology remains without clear parallel.

ln 89   The etymology is almost quite without parallel.
For "swallower", however, see Wutz, p. 251 and
material assembled there. The original spelling was doubtless with η "ɨ".

ln 90   Unparalleled etymology, based on בן + יה . A
different etymology for the name is Ona I ln
157.

ln 91   Ona I ln 172.

ln 92   No parallel in the lists. Compare Wutz, p. 327.
A transcription of the Hebrew measurement בת .

ln 93   Ona I ln 149.

ln 94   Ona I ln 170.

ln 95   The name and etymology do not occur in Ona I.
They are found in Greek, see the list printed
by Wutz, p. 681.

ln 96   Ona I ln 177.

ln 97   Ona I ln 166: slight difference in wording.

ln 98   The name and etymology do not occur in Ona I.
          They are found in Greek, see the list printed
          by Wutz, p. 709.

ln 99   Ona I ln 176: wording differs.

ln 100   The etymology does not occur elsewhere. For
          "ray", cf. "Barak" above. For "difficult,
          hard" no parallel is found.

ln 101   Cf. Ona I ln 174 <u>variae</u> <u>lectiones</u> with a dif-
          ference of wording. See very close Greek par-
          allel, Wutz, p. 713.

ln 102   The name and etymology do not occur in Ona I or
          elsewhere in the lists. No clear basis for "of
          passings" can be found.

ln 103   No parallels exist in the Armenian or Greek
          lists. Compare the Latin, Wutz, p. 147.

ln 104   Ona I ln 150.

ln 105   No parallel in Wutz. Apparently etymology
          derives from בתי"ך.

ln 106   Ona I ln. 156.

ln 107   The reading "daughter" may be found in Ona I ln
          139. It is no less strange than the reading
          "house" of MS 55, which is a dittography of the
          following. This etymology belongs, presumably
          to "Bathsheba" and not to "Beersheba", although
          a different etymology is given for that name by
          Ona I ln. 152. The confusion is ancient, cf.
          Wutz, p. 691. Here, however, the alphabetical
          order indicates that it is independent of the
          Greek confusion and arose in Armenian.

ln 108   For this etymology, see Wutz, p. 775. The
          etymology of this name in Ona I varies.

ln 109   Ona I ln 154.

ln 110   The etymologies for this name are derived
          from בית זית or בית ציד . Ona I ln 173 reads
          Ἐλεου for Ἐλαιας. The origins of the pres-
          ent reading therefore remain obscure.

ln 111   In Wutz, p. 707 "house of mouth or pharynx"
          is found in Greek and slightly different
          readings occur elsewhere (see Wutz, Index,
          s.v.). The reading here derives from this by
          a corruption of φάρυγξ to φάραγξ "gully,
          ravine". Ona I ln 175 is based on a differ-
          ent Greek tradition.

ln 112   For the name, see the Latin quoted by Wutz,
          p. 475. No parallel to the etymology given
          here was found.

ln 113   No clear parallels to the etymology "treach-
          erous" were found. For "without yoke", com-
          pare the Latin list given by Wutz, p. 772
          absque iugo.

ln 114   i.e. Baal Peor; the etymology does not
          accord with that given in the other Onomasti-
          ca. It is based on the same interpretation
          as line 112, deriving from בעל and פער .

ln 115   The name and etymology have no parallel in
          the lists, but their origin is transparent.

ln 116   Ona I ln 134.

ln 117   Not in Ona I, but in Cyril of Alexandria,
          Wutz, p. 1059 and Latin, Wutz, p. 579.

ln 118 Not in Ona I or Greek. For Latin parallel, see Wutz, p. 118, n. 1.

ln 119 Cf. Ona I ln 144.

ln 120 The name occurs with a different etymology in Ona I, ln 139. For this etymology, see Syriac list (Wutz, p. 793) and Theodoret (Wutz, p. 1061).

ln 121 Cf. Wutz, p. 649.

ln 122 Wutz, p. 346.

ln 123 See ln 89 for the etymology. The name is unknown in this form.

ln 124 Ona III ln 98.

ln 125 Ona I ln 167.

ln 126 The name also occurs in Ona I, but with a different etymology.

ln 127 Ona III ln 99.

ln 128 The name occurs elsewhere, e.g. Ona III ln 101, but the etymology remains without parallel.

ln 129 Ona III ln 103.

ln 130 "Gat'" 55: cf. Ona III ln 105 with different wording. With "arriving quickly", compare Wutz, pp. 689, 720.

ln 131 Cf. Ona III ln 104: wording differs.

ln 132 No parallels to the etymology are evident. It derives from a common meaning of ג״זל.

ln 133 Ona III ln 113: wording differs.

ln 134   i.e. "Galatians";   no parallels to the ety-
          mology are evident.

ln 135   Cf. Ona III ln 112.

ln 136   Cf. Ona III ln 115:   wording is different.

ln 137   Cf. Ona III ln 116:   wording is quite differ-
          ent.

ln 138   Or "breast":   Ona III ln 123.

ln 139   Ona III ln 117:   some difference of wording.

ln 140   Ona I ln 209:   Ona III ln 120 varies.

ln 141   No etymology is given for the name by either
          MS 55 or MS 81.

ln 142   Ona III ln 127 has the same etymology but a
          different word.   Compare ln 24 _supra_.

ln 143   Ona III ln 129.

ln 144   Compare Ona III ln 124:   see also Wutz, pp.
          169 f.

ln 145   This is apparently a variant for "Gomer", cf.
          Ona III ln 130, Ona I ln 207.

ln 146   Cf. Ona III ln 131, with a variant of the
          name.

ln 147   Ona I ln 264 _apparatus_ _criticus_.

ln 148   Ona III ln 133:   different wording.

ln 149   Ona III ln 135.

ln 150   Ona III ln 134:   different wording.

ln 151   Ona III lns 136-137.

ln 152   Ona III ln 138.

ln 153   Ona III ln 139.

ln 154   Ona III ln 140: wording differs.

ln 155   Ona III ln 142: wording differs somewhat.

ln 156   Ona III ln 143.

ln 157   Ona III ln 144: the genitive case is under-
          standable in Ona III but not in the present
          list.

ln 158   This etymology occurs in both Greek and Latin
          sources, see Wutz, p. 650.

ln 159   The etymology lacks in both manuscripts.

ln 160   Ona III ln 150.

ln 161   Not in Ona III; cf. in general Ona I, ln 247
          and apparatus criticus there, Wutz, p. 618.
          The meaning "judger (or: judging)" is unparal-
          leled.

ln 162   Ona III ln 149. The spelling of MS 55 is
          clearly required by the alphabetical order.

ln 163   Ona III ln 154: different wording.

ln 164   "Generation" in the sense of "origin", cf. Ona
          III ln 152.

ln 165   Ona III ln 153.

ln 166   See Ona III ln 198: Compare Wutz' important
          comments, p. 381. The parallels support the
          reading "of antiquity"of MS 55 rather than
          հնազանդութեան "of obedience" of MS 81. This
          is probably an inner-Armenian development.

ln 167   Ona III lns 325-326.

ln 168   i.e. "Hebrew"; Ona III ln 322: the ⟨ "h" in Ona III lns 322, 325-6 suggests a non-Greek origin there.

ln 169   The word ὑնηηιաδp "afflictions" is rare. The name and etymology do not appear in II and III. Compare, however, Ona I ln 282.

ln 170   Ona III ln 200.

ln 171   Ona III ln 201.

ln 172   Ona III ln 202 "red" (different word); cf. ln 27 above.

ln 173   Ona III ln 203.

ln 174   In Ona III ln 204 we read "god's help", cf. Ona II ln 27. The reading here accords with ln 172 and with the examples on Wutz, p. 807 ln 24, p. 829 ln 112, p. 1001 ln 23, et al.

ln 175   Cf. Ona III ln 242: difference in wording.

ln 176   Ona III ln 204.

ln 177   The name is perhaps parallel to that found in the Latin material quoted by Wutz, p. 781, but if so, then the etymologies are quite different. From the etymology, one might assume that the form of the name was "Ezron" חγ+ רון. If so, compare Ona I ln 275, and חצרון (Wutz, Index, s.v.). The etymology here is unknown although some analogous forms exist.

ln 178   Cf. Ona III ln 206: difference in wording.

ln 179   With the latter part of the etymology, cf. Origen quoted by Wutz, p. 740. No clear parallels to the first part occur in Wutz.

ln 180   This etymology, based on אל + קנא is quite
          different from that found in the Greek sources
          listed by Wutz or in Ona I ln 302. No paral-
          lels are to be found.

ln 181   See Ona I ln 302, 444; Wutz, p. 515. "Mercy"
          is unusual.

ln 182   Ona III ln 214.

ln 183   Ona III ln 213.

ln 184   Ona III ln 213.

ln 185   Ona III ln 217: difference in wording.

ln 186   This name does not appear in any of the sources
          adduced by Wutz nor in the Bible or New Testa-
          ment. The etymology is obvious.

ln 187   Ona III ln 224. Note there the non-Armenian
          form of the name.

ln 188   Ona III ln 215.

ln 189   Ona III ln 207: difference in wording. The
          reading "Eklisiastikēs" is apparently inner-
          Armenian.

ln 190   Ona III ln 235.

ln 191   Ona III ln 237.

ln 192   There appear to be no parallels to the name or
          etymology.

ln 193   Ona III ln 239.

ln 194   Ona III ln 165.

ln 195   The etymology appears to be without any paral-
          lel. Contrast Ona III ln 166.

ln 196   Ona III ln 168.

ln 197   Ona III ln 241.

ln 198   Ona III ln 170: slight difference in word-
              ing.

ln 199   This name is omitted by MS 81 and is out of
              alphabetical order in MS 55. It does not
              occur in the other Armenian onomastica, but
              the name is found in Latin quoted by Wutz,
              p. 482. The etymology is quite obvious.

ln 200   Ona III ln 422: "lord's mercy". The read-
              ing "god's" seems more accurate.

ln 201   Ona III ln 424.

ln 202   Ona III ln 425: difference in wording.

ln 203   Ona III ln 256.

ln 204   Cf. Ona I ln 268: difference in wording.

ln 205   Ona III ln 245: difference in wording.

ln 206   Ona III ln 177: slight difference in word-
              ing.

ln 207   For "dust", cf. Ona III ln 246. For the
              full etymology given here, see Wutz, p. 263.

ln 208   Ona III ln 180: difference of wording.

ln 209   Ona III ln 183: there the form is "Zambri".

ln 210   Ona III ln 187.

ln 211   Ona III ln 188.

ln 212   Ona III ln 189: difference of wording.

ln 213   So Jerome, see Wutz, pp. 481 ff. Contrast
              Ona III ln 191.

ln 214   Ona III ln 193: difference of wording.

ln 215   Ona III ln 197: complete difference in wording.

ln 216   Cf. Ona III ln 208.

ln 217   Ona III ln 250: difference of wording.

ln 218   No parallels to the etymology are found in Wutz' materials.

ln 219   Ona III ln 253.

ln 220   Cf. Ona III ln 254; Ona I ln 391; Wutz,p.195.

ln 221   Ona III ln 256.

ln 222   The spelling "T'ap'or" (MS 55) is demanded by alphabetical order, although "T'abor" (MS 81) is more correct. See Ona III ln 248.

ln 223   Corrupt in both copies for "T'erap'im": see Ona III lns 259–260.

ln 224   The spelling restored is that apparently demanded by alphabetical order. The name occurs, with a different etymology, in Ona I ln 376. For etymology, cf. Wutz, p. 145, but there is no exact parallel. It derives doubtless from תבל .

ln 225   Ona III ln 261.

ln 226   No parallel to this name is found in Wutz, nor does it appear in Bible, unless it is corrupt.

ln 227   With certain hesitation, this resolution of the abbreviation is given. This abbreviation usually stands for "Israel". Here, however, it is apparently a corruption for Ιεζραηλ which appears in Ona I ln 619 as Ձեզրայէլ with the same etymology as here (see <u>apparatus</u>

criticus in loc.) and compare also Ona III
ln 417. A form such as ﬗﬗﬗﬗ would also
appear to be demanded by alphabetical order
at this point and "Israel" appears immediately
following here ln 231. No such etymology
appears in the abundant sources for "Israel"
quoted by Wutz, pp. 88-90.

ln 228   Cf. Ona III ln 267. The same strange rendering of "T'amar" as "branch", noted on ln 207
supra, recurs here. No parallels were found.

ln 229   Ona III ln 270: difference in wording.

ln 230   Ona III ln 271: note similar inclusion of
ﬗ "is" in both lists, but difference in
wording.

ln 231   Ona III ln 274: difference in wording.

ln 232   For "seer of God", cf. Ona III ln 275. The
exact wording of the phrase occurs in Ona I
ln 414. For "vanquisher, of God" no parallel
is to be found in all the material assembled
by Wutz. The etymology is drawn, of course,
from Gen 32:28.

ln 233   Ona III ln 347: difference in wording.

ln 234   Ona III ln 285.

ln 235   Ona III ln 286.

ln 236   Ona III ln 287: difference in wording.

ln 237   Ona III ln 320: This is the same item,
contrast Ona III ln 76.

ln 238   Ona III ln 288.

ln 239   Ona III ln 290.

ln 240   Ona III   ln 292.

ln 241   Ona III   ln 293.

ln 242   Ona III   ln 685.

ln 243   Ona III   ln 296.

ln 244   Ona III   ln 297:   difference in wording.

ln 245   The name is apparently missing from the mate-
           rial assembled by Wutz. It is, in fact, an
           Armenian word meaning "heap of stones". Com-
           pare Ona III   ln 110 *Գալաադ. կարկառ վկայութեան*
           "Galaad, heap (karkaṙ) of witness".

ln 246   Ona III   ln 298.

ln 247   Cf. Ona III   ln 300. Wutz' rendering of
           պանդխտութեան   as "consolationis" is bizarre.

ln 248   Ona III   ln 301.

ln 249   Ona III   ln 302.

ln 250   Ona III   ln 694.

ln 251   Ona III   ln 304.

ln 252   Ona III   ln 306.

ln 253   Alternatively "difficult":   cf. Ona III   ln 309
           with different wording.

ln 254   The spelling of the name in MS 81 accords with
           alphabetical order. The etymology given here
           may be compared with Ona III   ln 311 *փառք ամի.*
           "glory of all". The present reading appears
           to have arisen through inner-Armenian confusion
           of two abbreviations.

ln 255   Ona III   ln 308.

ln 256   Ona III   ln 310:   difference in wording.

ln 257   i.e. "Colossians"; or "of desire": Compare
          Ona III ln 313: the etymology there differs
          somewhat.

ln 258   Ona III ln 312: difference in wording.

ln 259   For "bald" compare Ona III ln 316, Ona I ln
          448. The other etymologies are to be found in
          Ona III ln 315, where the name is spelt
          "Kōrē" in Ona III, while the form "Korx" oc-
          curs in Ona I. In our text קרח and קרא have
          been combined.

ln 260   i.e. Armenia; the name "Ararat" and its ety-
          mology occur in Ona III lns 77-78. The form-
          ulation found here does not occur in the other
          Armenian lists.

ln 261   Ona III ln 331: this word disrupts the al-
          phabetical order.

ln 262   Ona III ln 327: wording is quite different.

ln 263   Ona III ln 328.

ln 264   i.e. India; there is no parallel to this name
          in the Armenian lists. It may be compared
          with Latin "Supher", which is, in one list,
          equivalent to "Ophir" in etymology: see Wutz,
          p. 467. It seems likely that the correct
          reading is "Ophir", but the corruption may be
          pre-Armenian. This word occurs in Ona I, ln
          674, Ona III ln 517. No possible basis for
          the etymology given by the list here suggests
          itself.

ln 265   i.e. Indians; cf. Ona III ln 269: The ety-
          mology derives from the Hebrew הודו which was,
          presumably, included at some stage of the
          transmission. In Ona III the name is transli-

terated.

ln 266   Ona III   ln 337:   wording is quite different.

ln 267   i.e. Rome;   Ona III   ln 556:   the name in Ona
          III is simply a transliteration of Latin and
          the form դերամբարձ there is presumably cor-
          rupt.

ln 268   Ona III   ln 554:   difference in wording and
          transliteration of the name.

ln 269   Ona III   ln 278.

ln 270   Ona III   ln 343.

ln 271   Ona III   ln 341.

ln 272   Ona III   ln 342:   the name, in both manu-
          scripts, appears in this form, not as "ɬapi-
          dot'".

ln 273   Or "laws": cf. Ona III   ln 284   Լէ օի· օրէն
          "Lēči.law".

ln 274   Ona III   ln 344.

ln 275   The reading of MS 55 is corrupt, cf. Hebrew
          לחי :   Ona III   ln 283:   different wording.

ln 276   Ona III   ln 345.

ln 277   A general resemblance to this reading may be
          observed in Ona III   ln 350, Ona I   ln 499.

ln 278   Ona III   ln 352.

ln 279   Here the spelling of MS 81 reflects the alpha-
          betical order, which is, in fact, disturbed by
          the intrusive -y- in ln 277.   The name is
          found in Ona III   ln 354, but there the ety-
          mology is corrupt and, apparently also dif-
          fers.   That occuring here is not paralleled

by any of those cited by Wutz, p. 272, and its
connection with the root מע״ף is far from obvious.

ln 280   Ona III   ln 358.

ln 281   Ona III   ln 359:   the alphabetical order is
somewhat disturbed at this point.

ln 282   i.e. Magdalene;   Ona III   ln 357.

ln 283   The etymology does not appear in Wutz' materials.   It is obviously derived through the Hebrew root   יק״ד so   מוקד (Isa 33:14, PS 102:4,
etc.)

ln 284   Cf. Ona III   ln 360.

ln 285   This name is apparently a somewhat corrupt
form of Malaliēl,Ona I   ln 521, Ona III   ln
361.   The etymologies in both cases cited con-
cord with the present in sense, but not in
wording.

ln 286   Cf. Ona III   ln 365:   the name there is spelt
"Malak'ōn".

ln 287   Ona III   ln 366:   difference in wording.

ln 288   Ona III   ln 367 bears a general resemblance to
this etymology.

ln 289   Ona III   ln 368.

ln 290   Ona III   ln 369.

ln 291   Ona III   ln 370.

ln 292   Ona III   ln 377.

ln 293   Ona III   ln 392:   in Ona III the name is
"Misē".

ln 294   Ona III ln 372: "Masep'at" Ona III;
"Masep'ay" 55.

ln 295   Ona III ln 371.

ln 296   Ona III ln 376: the alphabetical order indicates that both MSS are corrupt and should
read "Matt'ēos.

ln 297   Ona III ln 379.

ln 298   Ona III ln 380.

ln 299   Ona III ln 386: 55 reads "king, lord".

ln 300   Ona III ln 387.

ln 301   Ona III ln 388.

ln 302   Cf. Ona III ln 399 "Mik'ōł".

ln 303   Ona III ln 395 "Mip'ibōsēt': wording differs.

ln 304   Ona III ln 389.

ln 305   Cf. Ona III ln 390. The etymology there ex-
plains between which rivers this land is loca-
ted. In the present list, the Armenian translation of "Mesopotamia" is given as the etymology.

ln 306   Ona III ln 394: the identification with Kadēs does not occur there; see supra, ln 238.

ln 307-8 This and line 306 may be divergent forms of
the same name. With "Miłk'ay", cf. Ona I
ln 545 "Mełkea, queen"; ln 564 մեղիք
"king". Ln 308 is found in Ona III ln 396.
Observe the graphic similarity of արքայ
"king" and աղքատ "poor" in uncial script.
Note further that ln 307 disturbs the alphabetical order.

ln 309   Ona III   ln 397.

ln 310   Cf. Ona III   ln 393.

ln 311   Ona III   ln 398:   the text of our list is
              preferable.

ln 312   Ona III   ln 391.

ln 313   This presumably refers to a mena (measure),
              cf. Ona III   ln 400. Neither form of the word
              occurs in Ezek 38.

ln 314   Ona III   ln 401.

ln 315   The spelling of MS 55 is preferable: cf.
              Ona III   lns 402-403.   Two different words are
              involved   מצה and   משא .

ln 316   Ona III   ln 406:   different wording.

ln 317   Ona III   ln 357.

ln 318   So Ona I   ln 592:   contrast Ona III   ln 412.

ln 319   So Ona III   ln 264:   spelling of Ona III
              betrays transliteration.

ln 320   For the name, see Wutz, p. 779.   No parallels
              to the etymologies are obvious.   "Elevation"
              may derive from   על and "goat of field" from
              אי   and איל .

ln 321   Ona III   ln 413.

ln 322   Ona III   ln 414.

ln 323   Ona III   ln 408.

ln 324   For the etymology "Jerusalem" compare Wutz,
              p. 723.   The word rendered "kicking" does not
              occur in the dictionaries, but is derived from
              a verb of this general meaning.   It should
              perhaps be compared with πεπατημένη (Origen,

apud Wutz, p. 745), and καταπατούμενος
(Wutz, p. 839) Ona III ln 416. These exact
etymologies do not occur in the other Armenian
lists.

ln 325   Ona III ln 334.

ln 326   This is apparent by a corrupt form of Ish-
            Bosheth, cf. Ona III ln 272.

ln 327   Ona III ln 433.

ln 328   Cf. Ona III ln 430.

ln 329   Ona III lns 431-432.

ln 330   Ona III ln 41b.

ln 331   Ona III ln 418: the etymology "offering" is
            not found there. For it, see the texts quoted
            by Wutz, pp. 774, 1023.

ln 332   Ona III ln 420.

ln 333   Ona III ln 426.

ln 334   This name not in Ona III: it occurs in Ona I
            ln 611 with a different etymology. For that
            given here, see Wutz, p. 255, etc.

ln 335   Ona III ln 434.

ln 336   Ona III ln 420.

ln 337   Ona III ln 428: different wording.

ln 338   Ona III ln 427.

ln 339   For "lamenter", MS 81 reads ωրρեgoη "drinker",
            perhaps an inner-Armenian variant: see Ona III
            ln 450.

ln 340   Ona III ln 439.

ln 341   The word ppɯnɯ does not occur in the dictionaries. It is perhaps to be connected with the
word ppnLɯ "earth". This name occurs in Ona
III ln 440 with a different etymology and
there are no other clear parallels.

ln 342   Ona III ln 453.

ln 343   Ona III ln 441.

ln 344   Ona III ln 443.

ln 345   Ona III lns 444-445.

ln 346   The reading "Yovakim" of MS 81 is corrupt as
is indicated by line 342 above where it occurs,
by the alphabetical order which it disturbs
and by the etymology itself. The etymology
occurs in Ona III ln 427 for another form of
this name "Yek'onias".

ln 347   Ona III ln 437.

ln 348   Cf. Ona III ln 451; "just" does not occur
there, nor is it usual with this name. Compare
ln 351 below.

ln 349   This and the following two names are only to
be found in MS 55. With this, contrast Ona III
ln 454 and see abbreviation above on ln 17.

ln 350   The incorrect "Yovnadan" of the MS has been
emended: compare Ona III ln 455 with
different wording.

ln 351   Compare this with ln 348, supra, these being
variant forms of the same name.

ln 352   Ona III ln 456.

ln 353   Ona III ln 458.

ln 354   Ona III   ln 459.

ln 355   Ona III   ln 265: wording differs.

ln 356   Not in the Armenian lists: compare the mater-
            ials in Wutz, p. 375, n.1.

ln 357   Ona III   ln 460.

ln 358   Ona III   ln 438.

ln 359   Ona III   ln 446: more correct spelling
            "Yoak'az" in Ona III.

ln 360   The form "Yewayim"   is doubtless corrupt for
            "Yewanim". Contrast Ona III   ln 415. No
            clear parallels occur in Wutz. The etymology
            doubtless derives from the Hebrew root ינ"ה .

ln 361   See Ona III   ln 475: This should probably be
            restored as Նաասոն "Naason".

ln 362   Ona III   ln 462.

ln 363   Ona III   ln 463: different wording.

ln 364   Ona III   ln 465: the etymology "pit" is not
            found there, nor elsewhere in Wutz' materials.

ln 365   Ona III   ln 466: different wording.

ln 366   Ona III   ln 471.

ln 367   Ona III   ln 472.

ln 368   Ona III   ln 473.

ln 369   Ona III   ln 474: MS 55 adds "Nayin, god's
            offering", a reading obviously conflated of
            lns 367-368.

ln 370   Cf. Ona III   ln 461: from Hebrew נאים .
            Contrast Ona I for this word, derived from
            נעים.

ln 371   Ona I   ln 664.

ln 372   Ona III   ln 476.

ln 373   Compare the material assembled by Wutz, p.498,
            where analogous etymologies are found; for the
            name, see Ona III   ln 481.

ln 374   Ona III   ln 478.

ln 375   Ona III   ln 482.

ln 376   Ona III   ln 479.

ln 377   A name otherwise attested only in Latin, cf.
            Wutz, p. 329.

ln 378   Ona III   ln 483:   different wording.

ln 379   Ona III   ln 484.

ln 380   Ona III   ln 485.

ln 381   Ona III   lns 486-487:   different wording.

ln 382   Some corruption of Hebrew במדבר lies behind
            this reading. No parallels occur in Wutz.

ln 383   One III   ln 565-566.

ln 384   Ona III   ln 651.

ln 385   Ona III   ln 501.

ln 386   Ona III   ln 494.

ln 387   A similar name Ոլլ "Ula" (as in MS 81)   with
            this etymology does not appear in Wutz' mater-
            ials. It may perhaps be derived from חיל or
            איל .. More likely, however, is the view that
            it is an inner-Armenian corruption of $q > \iota\iota$ ·
            In MS 55 Ոզ "Oza" is found, but there has
            been a hmt. which has resulted in the loss of
            the latter part of ln 385 plus the first part

of line 386. With this form, compare Ona III
ln 490.

ln 388   Cf. Ona III   lns 490, 492.

ln 389   Ona III   ln 493.

ln 390   Cf. Ona III   ln 495:   different wording.

ln 391   No ready parallels to this name can be ob-
          served in Wutz, nor does it appear in the
          Bible.

ln 392   In MS 81 there is a corruption of $\underline{\eta}$ > η. The
          reading of MS 55 shows its frequent shift of
          η "d" to θ "t'":   Ona III   ln 497.

ln 393   Ona III   ln 499.

ln 394   Ona III   ln 500.

ln 395   Ona III   ln 703.

ln 396   Ona III   ln 508.

ln 397   Ona III   ln 512:   MS 81 is corrupt.

ln 398   Corrupt form of the Hebrew name of this book.

ln 399   Ona III   ln 515.

ln 400   The name does not appear in Ona III.   In Ona I,
          ln 685, it occurs with a different etymology.
          For that here, cf. Ona III ln 90.   It is found
          in the material cited by Wutz, p. 517.

ln 401   Ona III   ln 518:   different wording.

ln 402   Ona III   ln 521.

ln 403   Ona III   ln 520.

ln 404   Ona III   ln 530.

ln 405   Ona III   ln 524.

ln 406   Ona III   ln 333.

ln 407   Cf. Ona III   ln 536 "Rabba".

ln 408   Ona III   ln 541.

ln 409   Ona III   ln 543:   different wording.

ln 410   Ona III   ln 535.

ln 411   Ona III   ln 544 "Ram".

ln 412   Ona III   ln 545.

ln 413   Ona III   ln 546.

ln 414   Ona III   ln 547.

ln 415   Ona I ln 705.

ln 416   Ona III ln 549

ln 417   Ona III   ln 551 and Ona I   ln 710 have this
           name, but each has an etymology different from
           the other, and both differ from that in the
           new list.   No parallels to the present etymo-
           logy may be found in Wutz.

ln 418   The name occurs in Ona III   ln 548 and other
           places (e.g. Wutz, pp. 92, etc.).   A possible
           alternative meaning for the word rendered
           "side" is "satiated", which might hesitantly
           be associated with Ona III ln 548 and the
           meaning multum accipiens, cf. Wutz, p. 469.

ln 419   The name occurs in Ona III   ln 552 with a
           different etymology.   A different sense of
           רכב   is behind Ona I   ln 713.   If Wutz n. on
           p. 986, is correct, the reading of Ona III
           ln 552 arises from an incorrect rendering of
           Latin quadriga.

ln 420   Ona III   ln 553.

ln 421   Ona III   ln 670: different wording.

ln 422   Ona III   lns 558-559.

ln 423   Ona III   ln 560: different wording.

ln 424   Saducees; Ona III   ln 574.

ln 425   Ona III   ln 577.

ln 426   Ona III   ln 578.

ln 427   Ona III   ln 579: different wording.

ln 428   Ona III   ln 581.

ln 429   Ona III   ln 582: different wording.

ln 430   Ona III   ln 587.

ln 431   The readings of MS 55 are to be preferred,
              particularly կրկնութիւն "repetition", for
              կրթութիւն "exercise" of 81: Ona III ln 595.

ln 432   The etymologies offered by the MSS here do not
              occur in Arm I or III. That of MS 55 եղեալ
              յաստուծոյ "placed by God" is analogous to
              material found in Wutz, p. 116, derived from
              שים and אל . No parallel to that of MS 81 is
              found.

ln 433   Ona III   lns 596-597.

ln 434   For "adversary", see Ona I ln 771. "Having
              borrowed" is not parallel and may go back to
              some corruption now beyond recovery.

ln 435   Ona III   ln 598.

ln 436   The word մակրրակ the etymology of "Sarona", is
              not found in the dictionaries. For the name,
              see Ona III ln 601.

ln 437   The reading *ѡηηιξυѡ*   of MS 55 is an
          inner-Armenian corruption: Ona III lns 602 -
          603.

ln 438   Ona III ln 605: the reading *Uѡփѡη* "Sap'ar"
          of Ona III is corrupt.

ln 439   Ona III 618.

ln 440   Ona III ln 627.

ln 441   Ona III ln 619.

ln 442   Ona III ln 606.

ln 443   Ona III ln 613 has the etymology "remaining",
          (using a different verb) and ln 621 has
          "peace-maker".

ln 444   Ona III ln 622.

ln 445   Cf. Ona I ln 747.

ln 446   Ona III ln 614.

ln 447   Ona III lns 624-625.

ln 448   This etymology is not recorded by Wutz.   It
          derives, of course, from סנה and חרב.

ln 449   Ona III ln 630.

ln 450   Ona III lns 628-619: "Sēiōra" of Ona III
          ln 629 is corrupt.

ln 451   Ona III ln 610: Ona III does not have
          "sender".

ln 452   Ona III ln 632: different wording.

ln 453   Ona III ln 633.

ln 454   Ona III ln 640: different wording.

ln 455   Ona III ln 641.

ln 456   Ona III   lns 642-643.

ln 457   Ona III   ln 646:   different wording.

ln 458   Ona III   ln 644.

ln 459   Ona III   ln 645 reads ϐϼι "number" which is,
            perhaps corrupt for ϐϭι "arm", a reading
            analogous to the present one, cf. Hebrew
            שכם.

ln 460   Ona III   ln 638.

ln 461   i.e. "Iscariot"; Ona III   ln 273.

ln 462   Ona III   ln 653.

ln 463   The spelling of MS 55, equivalent to Ona III
            ln 654, has been preserved.

ln 464   No parallels to this name or etymology appear.
            It is apparently derived from Latin somnus.

ln 465   Ona III   ln 648.

ln 466   Contrast Ona III   ln 655, which is a confused
            reading.

ln 467   Ona III   ln 652.

ln 468   No parallels are evident.

ln 469   Ona III   ln 255.

ln 470   Ona III   ln 661.

ln 471   Ona III   ln 662.

ln 472   Ona III   ln 663.

ln 473   Ona III   ln 664.

ln 474   Ona III   ln 666.

ln 475   Ona III   ln 671.

ln 476   The etymology is similar but not identical to
          those assembled by Wutz, p. 133.

ln 477   Ona III   ln 673.

ln 478   Ona III   ln 676.

ln 479   Ona III   lns 677-678.

ln 480   i.e. Pharisees; Ona III   ln 679.

ln 481   Ona III   ln 680:   different wording.

ln 482   Ona III   ln 684:   different wording.

ln 483   Compare Wutz, p. 430. Absent from Ona I, III.

ln 484   Ona I   ln 806:   different wording.

ln 485   Ona III   ln 685.

ln 486   The reading of MS 81 is clearly corrupt, cf.
          Ona I   850.   The etymology derives from   כזב .

ln 487   Cf. Ona I   ln 831.

ln 488   Ona III   ln 686:   different wording.

ln 489   Ona III   ln 687.

ln 490   Ona III   ln 323:   for "friendship", MS 81
          reads բարեբանութիւն "praise, benediction".

ln 491   Ona III   ln 303, cf. Ona II ln 45.

ln 492   Ona III   ln 338.

ln 493   Ona III   ln 339.

ln 494   Cf. Ona I   ln 835.

ln 495   Ona III   ln 697.

ln 496   Cf. Ona III   ln 335.

ln 497   Ona III   ln 698.

VI

ONA VI

i. Sample of Forty Names

1. Աբբանայ.   քար որոց երկրպագէին կամ կոչ տուն կամ
                     բաղալիք կամ լուացման տեղիք:

2. ✓ Աբբոր.   պահանորդ:

3. Աբղլմեհ.   ծառայ քրիստոսի:

4. Աբեղայ.   սգաւոր կամ տեւաւոր:

5. Աբիան.   աղքատ:

6. Աբրայ.   բարկացումն:

7. Ագապէն.   սիրուն:

8. Ագապ.   սէր:

9. ագահ.   անյագ:

10. Ագաթանգեղոս.   բարի հրեշտակ:

11. Ագաթիմովթ.   նղենի խլեալ {marg բք}:

12. ագարակ.   անդ կամ փոքր գիւղ:

13. ագանել.   օթեւանիլ կամ զգենուլ:{marg ի}

14. Ագազ.   երինջք:

15. ագասութիւն.   կոշումն:

16. Ագանովթայ.   անոթ երաժշտի կամ գործի:

17. Ագդէն.   թիւրադարձ:

18. ագելույն.   հագնելոյ յոտս:

19. Ագոն.   մրցութեան հրահանգ:

20. ագորանք.   մթերք աղբոյ:

1.   Abbanay,   a stone which they worshipped, or house
                   of idols or ⌈   ⌉ or places of
                   ⌈   ⌉.

2.   Abbor,   guard.

3.   Abdlmseh,   servant of Christ.

4.   Abełay,   mournful or black.

5.   Abian,   poor.

6.   Abray,   anger.

7.   Agapēn,   lovable.

8.   Agap,   love.

9.   Agah,   avaricious.

10. Agat'angełos, good angel.

11. Agat'r̓imovt', uprooted pomegranate tree {marg:
                   trees}

12. Agarak,   field or small village.

13. Aganel,   to lodge or to dress.

14. Agag,   heifer.

15. Agasut'iwn,   call.

16. Aganovt'ay,   instrument of music or work.

17. Agdēn,   false return.

18. Ageloyn,   of putting on the feet.

19. Agon,   instruction in wrestling.

20. Agorank',   heaps of dung.

21. Ազոր.   պահանորդ կամ թարձրութիւն:

22. Ագունիա.   ծածուկ:

23. պգււ.   գոգ կամ ազաբողոն:

24. Ադամայ.   եւ սիրոյ իմոյ ի Ե. քաղաքացն
                     սողոմայ:

25. Ադին.   ուրախութիւն կամ փափկութիւն:

26. Ադիալիպտոս.   անձանձրոյթ:

27. Ադոնա.   տէր կամ ամէնակալ:

28. {[Ադ]ոնայի.   տէր բսի յ[եբր]այեցի լեզուն:}

29. Ադոն.   տէր կամ ենթակա կամ տանաւդ կամ խարիսխ:

30. Ադոնիայի.   տեառն իմոյ կամ թուոյ յոլովութիւն
                     մի է յանուանց աատուծոյ զոր երբեմն
                     եղ փոխանակ անուան Աատուծոյ
                     որ չորիւք քառկանայ
                     տառիւք:

31. Ադարմեղեկի.   . . .

32. Ադոնմոյ.   պարզ քառ:

33. պգագունն.   նուազ կամ տղեղ:

34. ագգ.   սեռ կամ ցեղ:

35. ագղող.   ուժեղ:

36. ագղր.   անդամ:

37. ագղեր.   թեզանի:

38. Ագղէովթ.   ծոր կամ ցամաք:

39. Ագեկայ.   արեզակն:

40. Ագմողղեւ.   չար դեւ:

21. Agor,   guard or height.

22. Agunia,   hidden.

23. Aguṙ,   hollow, or cloak.

24. Adamay,   and of my love; (one) of the five
                   cities of Sodom.

25. Adin,   joy, or delight.

26. Adialeptos,   indefagitable.

27. Adona,   lord, or omnipotent.

28. {[Ad]onayi,   lord is (thus) heard in the {He}brew
                   tongue.}

29. Adon,   lord, or subject, or bearer, or base.

30. Adoniayi,   of my lord, or plural in number. It is
                   one of the names of God which some-
                   times it (i.e. scripture) places in-
                   stead of the name of God which is com-
                   posed of four letters.

31. Adarmeɫeki,   . . .

32. Adonmoy,   simple word.

33. Azazun,   few, or ugly.

34. Azg,   generation, or tribe.

35. Azdoɫ,   strong.

36. Azdr,   limb.

37. Azder,   sleeve.

38. Azdēovt',   valley, or dry land.

39. Azeka,   sun.

40. Azmoldew,   bad demon.

1 որոց ﹜ որ | բաղանիք | լուցման տեղիք   4
Աբեղա   5 Աբիոն   9 om   10 ազարակք
13 օթեւանիլ   14 ազատութիւնք կոչունք   16 om
18 om   19 հրահանք   20 աղբոց   24 om
25 փափկութիւն կամ ուրախութիւն   27 կամ ﹜ om
28 om   29 om   30 om   31 Անրամէլիք
արքայութիւն   35 ազղուօղ   38 ազատովղ
40

ln 1   MS 64 ln 3:   the end is corrupt for բաղանագիք
            կամ լուացման տեղիք

            (MS 64 and One I ln 78).   No parallels to the
            first part of the etymology occur in Wutz, but
            perhaps a derivation from אבנ is involved.

ln 2   MS 64 ln 4;   the name does not occur in any of
            Wutz' lists nor is the etymology readily ex-
            plicable.

ln 3   MS 64 ln 8;   this is clearly the name and
            etymology of Ona III ln 7 which has been mis-
            read by Wutz as "Abdlmoeh".   He has not trans-
            lated the unmistakable քհ.as "of Christ".

ln 4   MS 64 ln 10;   Ona I ln 105 has "Abeła, mourn-
            ing."   No parallel to "black" appears and,
            incidentally, the form of the word is not
            listed in the dictionaries.

ln 5   MS 64 ln 16;   Ona III ln 12.

ln 6   MS 64 ln 26;   Ona I ln 110.   The same word
            appears with a different etymology in Ona III.

ln 7   MS 64 ln 30;   the form "Agapos" occurs in Ona
            I and III, each with a different etymology and
            not derived from the Greek stem invoked by MS
            64 and Ona VI.   No other parallels are quoted
            by Wutz.

ln 8   MS 64 ln 31;   the comments in the preceding
            note also apply to this item.

ln 9   MS 64 omits.

ln 10   MS 64 ln 32;   not in Wutz or the Bible.

ln 11   MS 64 ln 34;   Ona I ln 81 with different word-
            ing.

ln 12   MS 64 ln 33.

ln 13   MS 64 ln 35.

ln 14   MS 64 ln 36;   Ona I ln 17 apparatus, Ona II
          ln 9.

ln 15   MS 64 ln 37;   the word ազատութիւն a clearly
          Armenian formation, does not appear in the
          dictionaries.

ln 16   Not in MS 64 nor in Wutz. The word is drawn
          from LXX Isa. 42:24.   The form quoted is
          actually an Armenian oblique case, the way
          the word appears in the Armenian version of
          Isaiah.   It reflects Hebrew אגבות .

ln 17   MS 64 ln 40;   The name is not found in Wutz
          or the Bible.   The word given as an etymology
          is not found in any of the dictionaries, but
          is compounded of two known elements. S. Shaked
          has suggested that this might conceivably re-
          flect Pahlavi agdēn "impious", if "difficult
          return" could be interpreted eschatologically.

ln 18   MS 64 omits.

ln 19   MS 64 ln 42;   like items 7 and 8, this is a
          Greek word not found in Wutz' onomastic mater-
          ial.

ln 20   MS 64 ln 41;   this is a variant spelling of
          the word agořank'.

ln 21   MS 64 ln 45;   On the form, see Wutz, p. 959 n.
          where an original *Argob is suggested.   The
          form occurring here is found elsewhere with
          the etymology "height", see Ona I, p. 864
          apparatus, Ona II ln 7.   "Guard" is identical
          with the insoluble name "Abbor" in ln 2, above,
          and perhaps a graphic confusion and conflation

of readings are possible.

ln 22   MS 64 ln 44;   the name is without parallel
         and quite inexplicable.

ln 23   MS 64 ln 43;   the connection is apparently
         between the sense of aguṭ "hollow of hand"
         and the sense of gog "hollow, cavity". The
         relationship with ałaboron "cloak" is quite
         obscure.

ln 24   MS 64 omits. The reference is to Adma אדמה
         mentioned with Sodom and three other cities
         in Gen 10:19. The etymology, however, may
         be derived from the stem חמ"ד reflected in
         the name חמדן which, metathesized as
         is the translation in LXX Gen 36:36 (contrast
         L ʽαμαδα): cf. Wutz, p. 895 n. A striking
         example.

ln 25   MS 64 ln 51;   the etymology "delight" occurs
         in Ona I, p. 866 apparatus. "Joy" is not
         found elsewhere.

ln 26   MS 64 ln 52;   deriving from Greek ἀδιάλειπτος .
         Occurs six times in the LXX and six times in
         the NT. No particular reason for its selec-
         tion for transliteration can be seen.

ln 27   MS 64 ln 54;   See Ona I ln 74, Ona III ln 29,
         Ona V ln 28 for the name and the etymology
         "lord". The reading "omnipotent" appears to
         be expansionary in character like the read-
         ings in items 4 and 25.

ln 28   MS 64 ln 64;   a marg. note secunda manu. The
         etymology "lord" is more usually found for
         "Adon", so Ona I lns 74-75, Ona III lns 29-30
         Ona V lns 28-29. No clear parallel to the

gloss is found, but cf. ln 30.

ln 29   MS 64 omits. For the etymology, see Ona III
         ln 29.

ln 30   MS 64 omits; see Ona III ln 30 which also
         contain the gloss, except for the final
         phrase.

ln 31   MS 64 ln 59; for the name, see Ona I ln 71,
         and MS 64 has just the first word of the ety-
         mology given by Ona I. Ona VI omits the ety-
         mology and the form of the name seems corrupt.
         In the dictionary of Eremia vardapet only the
         name "Adarmeheki" is found. This is doubt-
         less to be related to Ararmeliki. The ety-
         mology given these resembles that given by
         Ona I for "Adam".

ln 32   MS 64 ln 55; this name is listed in Wutz'
         Index s.v. but does not occur in his text.
         Might it be corrupt for "Adovnoy" and does
         the strange etymology mean that it is singu-
         lar as opposed to the plural on ln 30?

ln 33   MS 64 ln 61; the basic meaning of this word
         is "dried up, withered" which is apparently
         extended to the meanings given here.

ln 34   MS 64 ln 68.

ln 35   MS 64 ln 69.

ln 36   MS 64 ln 70.

ln 37   MS 64 ln 71; H. Ačaryan in his etymological
         dictionary of the Armenian language, s.v.
         quotes the apparently identical Ազդիր known
         only from the dictionary of Eremia vardepet
         with this same meaning. See: Armenian Ety-

<u>mological Dictionary</u>, Vol. I, Erevan: 1971,
(in Armenian), but on the meaning of the witness, see: Introductory Remarks, <u>supra</u>.

ln 38   MS 64 ln 72; no clear origin for the name or
           its etymology was found.

ln 39   MS 64 ln 73; the name occurs with quite a
           different etymology in Wutz, p. 358 <u>et</u> <u>al</u>.

ln 40   MS 64 omits; The name is most probably cor-
           rupt for Ազմոդեւ "Azmodew", i.e. Asmodeus
           (A suggestion of N. Bogharian).

ii. Sample of letter "ben"

1. *Բաբայ.*   *բլուր:*

2. *Բաէլ.*   *մանաւոր կամ խառնակութիւն:*

3. *Բաալ.*   *կուրք կամ տիրող:*

4. *Բաադ.*   *պատերազմեցաւ Աստուած:*

5. *Բաադիմ.*   *կուրք տիրողք:*

6. *Բաբելոն.*   *փոփոխումն կամ բաբել կամ խռովութիւն*
                   կամ խառնակութիւն բաբախել բախբախել:

7. *Բաթուէդ.*   *սիրելի աստուծոյ կամ զօրաւոր կամ*
                   որդիութիւն աստուծոյ կամ դուսար
                   աստուծոյ կամ կոյս:

8. *Բաթ.*   *միայն:*

ln 1   No parallels are evident.

ln 2   Perhaps corrupt for Babēl for which Ona V ln
          93 has "confusion". No explanation for
          "partial" can be seen.

ln 3   Ona V ln 85.

ln 4   Perhaps a corrupt remnant of an etymology for
          a name such as Jerubaal.

ln 5   Not in agreement with Ona I ln 165. It con-
          cords with Ona III ln 96 with some difference
          in wording.

1. Babay   hill.

2. Baēl,   partial, or mixture.

3. Baal,   idol, or master.

4. Baaɫ,   god fought.

5. Baaɫim,   idols, masters.

6. Babelon,   change, or Babylon, or confusion,

                     or mixture, to palpitate, to palpi-

                     tate.

7. Bat'ueɫ   beloved of god, or general, or

                     sonship of god, or daughter of god,

                     or virgin.

8. Bat',   alone.

ln 6   "Change --- mixture" are drawn from Ona I ln
            130 apparatus. There follow two spellings of
            a word "to palpitate" for which etymology
            there are no known parallels.

ln 7   "Daughter --- virgin" are drawn from Ona I ln
            132 apparatus, cf. ln 185. In MS 55 of Ona V
            "sonship of God" is to be found. "Beloved of
            god or general" remain unexplained.

ln 8   Ona I ln 187.

VII

List of Manuscripts

1. Codex Ticinensis (Pavia), II 2, 12 cent.
(Wutz, 849)

2. Berlin, Petermann 145, fols. 3r–33v, 1602
(Wutz, 849; Karamianz, no. 79)

3. Berlin, Minutius 273, fols. 2r–17v, 1618
(Wutz, 849; Karamianz, no. 80)

4. Vienna, Mechitarist no. 337, fols. 137r–158r, 15 cent.
(Wutz, 849)

5. Paris, Bibliothèque Nationale, MS Arm 302, fols. 79–93r, 13 cent.
(Wutz, 849)

6. Paris, Bibliothèque Nationale, MS Arm 271, fols. 111v–119v, 17 cent.
(Wutz, 849)

7. Paris, Bibliothèque Nationale, MS Arm 260, fols. 1–32r, 16 cent.
(Wutz, 849)

8. Vienna, Bibl. Aul. Cod. Arm., fols. 108r–118v, 1683
(Wutz, 849)

9. Vienna, Mechitarist, no. 319, fols. 312v–325v, 1697
(Wutz, 962)

10. Erevan, Matenadaran, no. 2371, Surxat', 1357
(Catalogue 1,789)

11. Erevan, Matenadaran, no. 4149, Erznka, 1304–05
(Catalogue 1,1157)

12. Erevan, Matenadaran, no. 5596, 13 cent.
(Catalogue 2,141)

13. Erevan, Matenadaran, no. 5925, Varag (?), 15 cent.
(Catalogue 2,213)

14. Erevan, Matenadaran, no. 8198, 14 cent.
(Catalogue 2,693)

15. Erevan, Matenadaran, no. 266, 1468
(Catalogue 1,285)

16. Erevan, Matenadaran, no. 267, 1609, 1613
                              (Catalogue 1,285-6)

17. Erevan, Matenadaran, no. 516, 17 cent.
                              (Catalogue 1,338-9)

18. Erevan, Matenadaran, no. 530, Jagavank', 14 cent.
                              (Catalogue 1,342)

19. Erevan, Matenadaran, no. 534, 17 cent.
                              (Catalogue 1,343)

20. Erevan, Matenadaran, no. 536, 17 cent.
                              (Catalogue 1,343)

21. Erevan, Matenadaran, no. 538, 1595
                              (Catalogue 1,343-4)

22. Erevan, Matenadaran, no. 843, Toxat', 18 cent.
                              (Catalogue 1,423)

23. Erevan, Matenadaran, no. 2019, Julfa, 1600
                              (Catalogue 1,701)

24. Erevan, Matenadaran, no. 2291, Caesaria, 1665
                              (Catalogue 1,768)

25. Erevan, Matenadaran, no. 2330, Kaffa, 1633, 1641-43
                              (Catalogue 1,776-7)

26. Erevan, Matenadaran, no. 2331, 17 cent.
                              (Catalogue 1, 777)

27. Erevan, Matenadaran, no. 2335, Jerusalem, 1476
                              (Catalogue 1, 779)

28. Erevan, Matenadaran, no. 2369, Constantinople, 1614
                              (Catalogue 1, 788)

29. Erevan, Matenadaran, no. 2370, Constantinople,
    1621-24   (Catalogue 1,788-9)

30. Erevan, Matenadaran, no. 2372, 16 cent.
                              (Catalogue 1, 789)

31. Erevan, Matenadaran, no. 2381, Yovhannavank', 1631
                              (Catalogue 1, 791)

32. Erevan, Matenadaran, no. 3170, 17 cent.
(Catalogue 1,955)

33. Erevan, Matenadaran, no. 3197, 16 cent.
(Catalogue 1,961)

34. Erevan, Matenadaran, no. 3200, 17 cent.
(Catalogue 1,962)

35. Erevan, Matenadaran, no. 3201, St. James, 1419
(Catalogue 1,962)

36. Erevan, Matenadaran, no. 3202, 1417
(Catalogue 1,962)

37. Erevan, Matenadaran, no. 3261, 17 cent.
(Catalogue 1,975)

38. Erevan, Matenadaran, no. 3937, 1370
(Catalogue 1,1114)

39. Erevan, Matenadaran, no. 4283, 1616(?)
(Catalogue 1,1184)

40. Erevan, Matenadaran, no. 4398, 17 cent.
(Catalogue 1,1205)

41. Erevan, Matenadaran, no. 5008, Tak'irdat, 1623-43
(Catalogue 2,15)

42. Erevan, Matenadaran, no. 5919, 14 cent.
(Catalogue 2,211)

43. Erevan, Matenadaran, no. 5947, 17 cent.
(Catalogue 2,217-8)

44. Erevan, Matenadaran, no. 5995, 17 cent.
(Catalogue 2,228-9)

45. Erevan, Matenadaran, no. 6624, 17 cent.: according
to Amalyan (p. 234) this contains the work,
but it is not listed in the contents in
Catalogue 2, 359-60.

46. Erevan, Matenadaran, no. 7014, Jerusalem, 17 cent.
(Catalogue 2,440-1)

47.   Erevan, Matenadaran, no. 7117, Mecop', 1440 (?)
                          (Catalogue 2,464-5)

48.   Erevan, Matenadaran, no. 7995, Istambul, 1632-3
                          (Catalogue 2,651)

49.   Erevan, Matenadaran, no. 8106, 16 cent.
                          (Catalogue 2,674-5)

50.   Erevan, Matenadaran, no. 8354, 17 cent.
                          (Catalogue 1,727)

51.   Erevan, Matenadaran, no. 8563, Constantinople, 1620
                          (Catalogue 2,772)

52.   Erevan, Matenadaran, no. 1921, 1732-3
                          (Catalogue 2,874)
            erroneously listed by Amlyan as no. 9112

53.   Venice, Mechitarist, no. 1409, pp. 1-26, notragir

54.   Venice, Mechitarist, no. 544, 14-15 cent., pp.1-30
            bolorgir

55.   Venice, Mechitarist, no. 545, 16-17 cent., pp.393-
            404

56.   Venice, Mechitarist, no. 39, pp. 120-137, notragir

57.   Jerusalem, Armenian Patriarchate, no. 657, fols.
            285r-343v, notragir (Catalogue 3, 86-8)

58.   Jerusalem, Armenian Patriarchate, no. 857, fols.
            101r-121v, notragir (Catalogue 3,348-9)

59.   Jerusalem, Armenian Patriarchate, no. 1004, fols.
            2r-29r, 1613, notragir (Catalogue 4,6-7)

60.   Jerusalem, Armenian Patriarchate, no. 1173, fols.
            3r-30v, 17 cent.   (Catalogue 4,272)

61.   Jerusalem, Armenian Patriarchate, no. 1666, fols.
            97r ff., 1642   (Catalogue 5, 5)

62.   Jerusalem, Armenian Patriarchate, no. 1672, pp. 5
            ff., 17 cent.   (Catalogue 5,527)

63. Jerusalem, Armenian Patriarchate, no. 1682, pp. 185
         ff., 1359   (Catalogue 5,543)

64. Jerusalem, Armenian Patriarchate, no. 1352, pp.297-
         504, Jerusalem, 1688   (Catalogue 4,625)

65. Jerusalem, Armenian Patriarchate, no. 2481, pp.122-
         149, 1306   (Catalogue 8,151)

66. Paris, Bibliothèque Nationale cod. arm. 140, fols.
         239v ff., notragir

67. Bzommar, no. 204, fols. 252v-260v, 1178
                                   (Catalogue 1, 486-495)

68. Bzommar, no. 227, fols. 173r-196r, 1410
                                   (Catalogue 1, 539-42)

69. Galata, no. 95 pp. 201-2 (alphabet)(Catalogue, 602)

70. Galata, no. 100, pp. 355-381, notragir
                                   (Catalogue, 630)

71. Tabriz, no. II 14 (alphabet, some names) 1678
                                   (Catalogue, 57)

72. Vienna, Mechitarist, no. 672, fols. 93r-121v,17 cent.
                                   (Catalogue 2, 166)

73. Vienna, Mechitarist, no. 1017, fols. 2r-16r, 17-18
         cent.   (Catalogue 2, 608)

74. Vienna, Mechitarist, no. 1124, fols. 188r-191v, 18
         cent.   (Catalogue 2,768-9)

75. London, British Library, MS or 6991, fols. 141-220,
         18 cent.   (Catalogue, 311)

76. London, British Library, catalogue no. 260, fols.
         1r-31r, 16 cent.   (Catalogue, 137)

77. Oxford, Bodleian Library, MS or e 27, fol. 194, 18
         cent.   (Catalogue, 758)

78. Jerusalem, Armenian Patriarchate, no. 1372, pp. 29–
         59   (Catalogue 5, 8–10)

79. Jerusalem, Armenian Patriarchate, no. 1008, pp.1–15
                                      (Catalogue 4, 11)

80. Jerusalem, Armenian Patriarchate, no. 1912,Kaffa(?),
         1369   (Catalogue 6,344)

81. Erevan, Matenadaran, no. 2261, fols. 300v–310v, 17
         cent.   (Catalogue 1,758)

82. Jerusalem, Armenian Patriarchate, no. 1422, fols.
         325r–613v, 17 cent. (Catalogue 5, 86)

83. Jerusalem, Armenian Patriarchate, no. 1448, fols.
         263r–310r, 1583   (Catalogue 5, 129)

84. Jerusalem, Armenian Patriarchate, no. 1699, pp.
         10–69, 17 cent.   (Catalogue 5, 574)

85. Bzommar, no. 549, fols. 15 ff., 16–17 cent.
                                      (Catalogue 2, 157)

86. Aleppo, 40 Martyrs, no. 72, pp. 5–48, 16 cent.
                                      (Catalogue, 152)

87. New Julfa, All-Saviour, no. 75, fols. 4f–33v, 1220
                                      (Catalogue, 837)

88. New Julfa, All-Saviour, no. 160, fols. 275–465,
         16–17 cent.   (Catalogue, 838)

89. Kurdian Collection, 18 century (Catalogue, 12)

90. Jerusalem, Armenian Patriarchate, no. 2523, pp.
         275–384, 17–18 cent. (Catalogue 8,199)

PART THREE

THE SONS OF NOAH

AND

THE GENERATIONS FROM ADAM

I

INTRODUCTORY REMARKS

The Peoples of the Sons of Noah

This text is based, ultimately, on Gen 10,2 Chr
1:5-21, both texts dealing with the enumeration of the
nations descending from the three sons of Noah and the
division of the earth among them. Other ancient sources
reflecting this tradition are, e.g. Jub. 7:13-19, Bib.
Ant. 4:1-10.

The document published here is drawn from Erevan,
MS No. 533, written in 1660 C.E. (Erevan Catalogue, 1,
cols. 342-43). It is particularly close to the material
parallel in content to be found in the Armenian version
of The Chronicle of Michael the Syrian. [1] A close parallel is also to be observed in the Syriac text of The
Chronicle. [2] An earlier stage of this tradition is to
be observed in The Cave of Treasures. [3]

A much expanded form of the same body of material,
in the section dealing with the descendants of Japheth,
may be observed in the second chapter of The History of
the Caucasian Albanians by Moses Dasxuranc'i. [4] In a
note to this passage, Dowsett points out that in it
Dasxuranc'i is dependent on the Chronicle by Hippolytus
which was published, in its Armenian version, by Sarghissian. [5] Chabot does not reckon Hippolytus' Chronicle among the sources used by Michael the Syrian, [6] and
a particularly close relationship exists between Michael's work and the text published here, as is indicated
at a number of points in the Commentary below. It thus
seems that there may be some intermediate link in the
transmission.

The Generations from Adam

        This is a chronological list by rulers, starting
from Adam and extending to the seventh century C.E. The
first figure following each name in this list indicates
the number of years which the designated person reigned.
The second of the two figures is a cumulative total. The
biblical ages generally follow the Septuagint reckoning,
where this differs from that of the massoretic text.
There are fairly frequent confusions and corruptions of
the numbers which have been signalled in the commentary
and, where possible, corrected in the text. In the
translation, the names have been given in their usual
English form where they could be clearly identified.
Unusual forms in Armenian are noted in the commentary.

        The work is found in Erevan, Matenadaran, No.8076,
fols. 221r-222r. This is a Miscellany of the 17th century, containing a good number of texts of interest for
study of the Pseudepigrapha. The Generations is not
listed by the Catalogue (Erevan Catalogue, 2. cols. 667-
668) and is followed by two pages of chronological sum-
maries which are not of great interest.

        The transliterations of names make it likely that
the list was translated into Armenian from Greek, and
such forms as Eɫisabos (ln 83),Iyovhannēs (lns 85,97),
the various corruptions of the name Onias (lns 87,90,93,
95), Ɩesus (ln 94), and others all reflect Greek spelling rather than the usual Armenian forms of the names.

        From its conclusion it is likely that the list was
composed in the middle of the seventh century C.E.;
Heraclius ruled from 610-641 (see ln 154) and was succeeded by his two sons, first Heraclius Constantinus,
the "Constantinus" of The Generations (ln 155), who
ruled for some months, and then Heracleonas who was
immediately overthrown by the army. Next ruled Constans
II (642-688), apparently the "Kostandin" of the text
(ln 156.) The Generations from Adam records only two

years for his reign seemingly implying that it was com-
pleted in his third year, i.e. 644 C.E.

էջ 234   ԱԶԳ ՈՐԴՈՑՆ ՆՈՅԻ

            1 ի Սեմայ։ եբրայեցիք. փոանկք. պարսիկք
               եւ այլք։
               Եւ է սահման Սեմայ։ ընդ

էջ 235   մէջ ձերկրեայս / յարեւելից եւ
               յարեւմտից. զպարսից աշխարհն.
               զասորոց. զպաղեստին. մինչեւ՝ի
               նեղոս գետ։

            2 Յաբեդի ազգք։ հայք.
               մակեդոնացիք. մադացիք. յոյնք.
               լատինացիք. ալանք. եւ վրացիք։ Եւ
               սահմանք յաբեդի է։ մադիէ մինչ
               ի գադիրոն Հիւսիսոյ.
               եւ արդ ունի ազգն աբեդի
               (յազեան) տիգրիս գետոյ
               որ բաժանէ ընդ մադէ եւ ընդ պարսս։

            3 Քամայ են։ եգիպտացիք. Հնդկացիք.
               Հեթացիք. յեփուսացիք. Հաբաշիք՛
               որք են քուշացիք. ամուրհացիք.
               գերգեսացիք. արուդացիք. քադդէացիք
               որք են ասորիք։
               Եւ սահման քամայ է։ զՀարաւ.
               եւ մանիտոն էառ յայն կոյս

The People(s) of the Sons of Noah

1 <u>From Shem</u>: the Hebrews, the Franks, the

Persians and others.

And the border of Shem is around the

middle part of the earth, to the east and

to the west; the land of the Persians,

that of the Syrians, Palestine as far

as the river Nile.

2 <u>The Nations of Japheth</u>: the Armenians, the

Macedonians, the Medes, the Greeks, the

Latins, the Alans and the Georgians. And

the border of Japheth is from Media to

Northern Gadiron;

and now the nation of Japheth holds

⌐one word⌐   of the Tigris river

which is between Media and Persia.

3 <u>Of Ham are</u>: the Egyptians, the Indians, the

Hittites, the Jebusites, the Habašites

who are the Cušites, the Amorites, the

Gergasites, the Arudites, the Chaldaeans

who are the Syrians.

And the border of Ham is to the south,

and he took Manitōn on the other side

ծովուն:

4 Յետ աւետեացն աստուծոյ առ աբրահամ

    ՆԼ ամ լինի մինչ ի յելան յեգիպտոսէ.

    ՄԵ մինչ ի գալն յակոբայ էր

    եւ ՄԻԵ մինչեւ

    ի յելան. բայց ճԽԴ ամ ի

    չարչարանս կային:

of the sea.

4 After the announcement of God to Abraham, there

   were 430 years up to the exodus from Egypt.

   There were 205 years up to the coming of

   Jacob (i.e. to Egypt) and 225 (from that

   time) until the exodus, but they were af-

   flicted for 144 years.

---

1 *եբրայեցիք* "the Hebrews": The list of peoples resembles that of <u>The Chronicle</u>, but that work places the
"Syrians" first. Contrast here 3 below.

մէջ. "the middle part of the earth". The idea is not
present in <u>The Chronicle</u>, but compare <u>The Cave of
Treasures</u> "und ihnen gehört der Mittelpunkt der Erde".

2 *հայք* "the Armenians": The Armenian version of The Chronicle also places the Armenians first. They are second in the Syriac.

Գադիրոն "Gadiron": So also Michael in The Chronicle, and Dasxuranc'i. Dowsett identifies it as Cadiz, and Chabot as Cadix. It is north of Media.

յազեան ⸢one word⸣: Apparently corrupt. The Armenian version of The Chronicle has *յակնէն* apparently a mediaeval form for classical *յականէն* "from the source of", while in Dasxuranc'i the sentence reads "from Media to Gadiron (Cadiz) in the north and down to the river Tigris which separates Media from Babylon" (tr. Dowsett, p.1). The Tigris, in fact, runs from Media and Babylon, as stated by Dasxuranc'i; the reading "Persia" of our text and The Chronicle is an important indication of their affiliation.

3 *քաղդէացիք* "Chaldeans": The Chaldeans and Syrians appear in The Chronicle among the descendants of Shem, see also Gen 10:22.

Ման իտոն--ծովուն "Maniton--sea": Quite inexplicable on the basis of The Chronicle.

4 This chronology is standard. The period of 430 years is found in Exod 12:40, cf. Gal 3:17. Dating by the promise to Abraham may be observed in The Chronicle, Chabot pp. 35 ff., but The Chronicle reckons 215 years from the descent into Egypt to the Exodus (p. 39) and its ages for Isaac and Jacob also produce this total for the period from the promise to Abraham up to the Exodus.

ԾՆՈՒՆԴՔ ՅԱԴԱՄԱՅ ԵՒ ԹԻՒՔ ՆՈՑԱ

221ա 1   Ադամ եկաց ՄԼ ամ եւ ծնաւ զՍԷԹ:

ՍԷԹ. ամս	ՄԵ միաւորեայ եւ լինի նԼԵ:	
Ենովս	ՃՂ	ՈԺԵ:
Կայինայն	ՃՀ	ՋԺԵ:
5 Մաղաղիէլ	ՃԿԵ	ՋԿ:
Յարեթ	ՃԿԲ	ՈՃԺԲ:
Ենովք	ՃԿԵ	ՈՄՂԵ:
Մաթուսաղայ	ՃԿԵ	ՈՆՕԲ:
Ղամէք	ՃԲ	ՈՈԼԴ:
10 Նոյ	Շ	ՍՃԼԴ:
Սեմ	Ճ	ՍՄԼԴ:
Արփաքսադ	ՃԼԵ	ՍՅՀՍ:
Կայինան	ՃԼ	ՍՇՍ:
Սաղայ	ՃԼ	ՍՈԼՍ:
15 Եբեր	ՃԼԴ	ՍՋԿԵ:
Փաղեկ	ՃԼ	ՍՊՂ
Ռագաւ	ՃԼԲ	ՍՋԻԷ:
Սերուք	ՃԼ	ՎԿԷ:
Նաքովր	ՀԹ	ՎՃԼՉ:
20 Թարայ	Հ	ՎՄՉ:
Աբրամ	Ճ	ՎՅՉ:
Իսահակ	Կ	ՎՆՀԲ:

THE GENERATIONS FROM ADAM AND THEIR NUMBERS

1	Adam lived	230 years and begot Seth	
	Seth	205, altogether	435
	Enosh	190	625
	Kenan	170	795
5	Mahalalel	165	960
	Jared	162	1,122
	Enoch	165	1,29<7>
	Methuselah	165	1,452
	Lamech	102	1,634
10	Noah	500	2,134
	Shem	100	2,234
	Arpachshad	137	2,371
	Kainan	130	2,501
	Shelah	130	2,631
15	Eber	134	2,765
	Peleg	130	2,89<5>
	Reu	132	2,927
	Serug	130	3,067
	Nahor	79	3,136
20	Terah	70	3,206
	Abraham	100	3,306
	Isaac	60	3,472

	Յակոբ	ԻԵ	ՎՇՁԲ:
	Ղելի	ԽՋ	ՎԿԵ:
25	Կաճաթ	Կ	ՎՈԿԵ:
	Ամրամ	Հ	ՎՁԼԵ:
	Մովսէս	Շ	ՎՊԺԵ:
	Յանապատն	Խ	ՎՊՁԵ:
	Յեսու Նաւեայ	ԻԵ	ՎՊՋ:
30	Փենիէս	ՄԴ	ՎՁԴ:
	Քուսարսադ	Ը	ՎՁԺՍ:
	Գողոնիէլ	Խ	ՎՁՁՍ:
	Եգղոմ	ԺԸ	ՎՁԿԹ:
	Աղովք եւ ամեկ	Շ	ՏԽԹ:
35	Աբիսացիբ	ի	ՏԿԹ:
	Դեբովրայ	Խ	ՏՁԹ:
	Ուբեք գեթ	Է	ՏՁՁՋ:
	Գեղեոն	Խ	ՏՁՁՋ:
	Աբիմելեբ	Գ	ՏՁՁԹ:
40	Թովղայ	իԴ	ՏՁ2Բ:
	Յայիր	իԲ	ՏՄԴ:
	Ամոնացիբ	ԺԸ	ՏՄիԲ:
	Յեփթայի	Ջ	ՏՄիԸ:
	Եսիբոն	Է	ՏՄԼԵ:
45	Աղղոնն	Ժ	ՏՄԽԵ:

	Jacob	85	2,55(2)
	Levi	46	(3,065)
25	Kohath	60	3,665
	Amram	70	3,735
	Moses	80	3,815
	In the desert	40	3,855
	Joshua b. Nun	25	3,880
30	Phineas	24	3,904
	(Cushan-Risha-thaim)	8	3,911
	Othniel	40	3,951
	Eglon	18	3,969
	Ehud and (Amalek)	80	4,049
35	Abisac'ik'	20	4,069
	Deborah	40	4,109
	Orēb, Zeeb	7	4,116
	Gideon	40	4,156
	Abimelech	3	4,159
40	Tola	24	4,182
	Jair	22	4,204
	Ammonites	18	4,222
	Jephtah	6	4,228
	Heshbon	7	4,235
45	Elon	10	4,245

	Աբդոն	Շ	ՏՄՃԳ:
	Փղշտացիք	Խ	ՏՄՂԴ:
	Սամփսոն	ի	ՏՅԺԴ:
	Անիշխան	Խ	ՏՅՃԴ:
50	Հեղի	ի	ՏՅՀԴ:
	Սամուէլ	ի	ՏՅՂԴ:
	Սաւուղ	Խ	ՏՆԺԴ:
	Դաւիթ	Խ	ՏՆՃԴ:
	Սողոմոն	Խ	ՏՆՂԴ:
55	Րոբովամ	ԺԷ	ՏՃԺ:
	Աբդիու	Գ	ՏՃԺԴ:
	Ասափ	ԽՍ	ՏՃՃԵ:
	Իյովսափաթ	իԵ	ՏՃՀԹ:
	Յովրամ	Շ	ՏՃՂԷ: /
211p			
60	Ոքոզիաս	Ս	ՏՃՂՇ:
	Գոթոդիաս	Է	ՏՃՀԵ:
	Յովաս	Խ	ՏՈՒԵ:
	Ամասիաս .	իԹ	ՏՈԿԴ:
	Ոզիաս	ԾՒ	ՏՉԺՁ:
65	Իյովաթամ	ԺՒ	ՏՉԼՁ:
	Աքազ	ԺՒ	ՏՉԽՐ:
	Եզեկիաս	իԹ	ՏՉՀԵ:
	Մանասէ	ԾՒ	ՏՊԼՁ:
	Ամովս	Ձ	ՏՊԼԴ:

	Abdon	8	4,253
	Philistines	40	4,294
	Sampson	20	4,314
	No ruler	40	4,354
50	Eli	20	4,374
	Samuel	20	4,394
	Saul	40	4,414
	David	40	4,454
	Solomon	40	4,494
55	Rehoboam	17	4,51<1>
	(Abijah)	3	4,514
	(Asa)	41	4,555
	Jehosaphat	25	4,579
	Joram	8	4,587 /
211v			
60	Ahaziah	1	4,588
	Athaliah	7	4,595
	Joash	40	4,635
	Amaziah	29	4,664
	Uzziah	52	4,716
65	Jotham	16	4,732
	Ahaz	16	4,748
	Hezekiah	29	4,77<7>
	Manasseh	52	4,832
	(Amon)	2	4,834

70	Յովսիայ	ԼԱ	ՏՊԿԵ։
	Յովաքազ	Ա	ՏՊԿՁ։
	Եղիակիմ	ԺԱ	ՏՊՀԷ։
	իյովակիմ	Ա	ՏՊՀԸ։
	Սեդեկիայ	ԺԱ	ՏՊՂԹ։
75	Նաբուգոթոնոսոր	ԺԱ	ՏՂԺ։
	Նիրիկդիաթ	Ե	ՏՂԺԵ։
	Բաղտասար	Գ	ՏՂԺԸ։
	Դարեհ Մար.	ԺԸ	ՏՂԼՁ։
	Կիւրոս	ԼԲ	ՏՂԿԸ։
80	Կամբիւսիոս	Ը	ՏՂՀՁ։
	Յեսու առաջնորդ.	ԼԲ	ՐԸ։
	իյովակիմ	Լ	ՐԼԸ։
	Եղիասիբոս	Խ	ՐՀԸ։
	Յովիդայէ	ԼՂ	ՐՃԺԴ։
85	իյովհաննէս	ԼԲ	ՐՃԽՁ։
	Աբեդուս	ի	ՐՃԿՁ։
	Աննինաս	իԲ	ՐՃՁԸ։
	Սիմոն	ԺԵ	ՐՄԵ։
	Աւնիաս	ԺԴ	ՐՄԺԹ։
90	Եղիազար	ԼԲ	ՐՄԾԱ։
	Մանասիս	իՂ	ՐՄՀԵ։

70	Josiah	31	4,865
	Jehoahaz	1	4,866
	Eliakim (Jehoiakim)	11	4,877
	Jehoiachin	1	4,878
	Zedekiah	11	4,889
75	Nebuchadnezzar	11	4,910
	Neriglissar	5	4,915
	Balthasar	3	4,918
	Darius the Mede	18	4,936
	Cyrus	32	4,968
80	Cambyses	8	4,976
	Joshua I	32	5,008
	Jehoiakim	30	5,038
	Eliashib	40	5,078
	Jehoiada	36	5,114
85	Johanan	32	5,146
	(Jaddua)	20	5,166
	Onias	22	5,188
	Simon	15	5,207
	Onias	14	5,219
90	Eleazar	32	5,251
	Manasseh	26	5,277

Սիմոն	իե	ՐՅԲ :
Իոնիաս	է	ՐՅիՁ :
Իեսուս	Ձ	ՐՅԼԲ :
95 Իոնիաս	է	ՐՅԼԹ :
Իոնիաթէս .	ժէ	ՐՅծՁ :
Սիմոն	Ը	ՐՅԿԴ :
իյովաննէս	Լ	ՐՅՂԴ :
Արիստաբուլոս	Ա	ՐՅՂԵ :
100 Աղեքսանդրոս	Թ	ՐՆԴ :
Յաննէոս	Լ	ՐՆԼԴ :
Հիւրկիասոս	ԼԴ	ՐՆԿԲ :
Հերովդէս	Դ	ՐՆՀԲ :
Յուլիոս	Դ	ՐՆՀՁ :
105 Աւգաստոս	ծՁ	ՐՇԼԲ :
Տիբերիոս	իԲ	ՐՇծԴ :
Գայիոս	Դ	ՐՇծԸ :
Կղոդիոս	ժԴ	ՐՇՀԲ :
Ներոն	ժՂ	ՐՇՁԵ :
110 Վէսպիանոս	ժ	ՐՇՂԵ :
Տիտոս	Գ	ՐՇՂՁ :
Դոմետիանոս	ժ	ՐՈՁ :
Տրայիանոս	ժԹ	ՐՈիէ :
Անդրիանոս	իԱ	ՐՈխՁ :

	Simon	25	5,302
	Onias	7	5,326
	Jesus	6	5,332
95	Onias	7	5,339
	Ioniat'ēs	17	5,356
	Simon	8	5,364
	Johanan	30	5,394
	Aristobulos	1	5,395
100	Alexander	9	5,404
	Jannaeus	30	5,434
	Hyrcanus	34	5,468
	Herod	4	5,472
	Julius	4	5,476
105	Augustus	56	5,532
	Tiberius	22	5,554
	Gaius	4	5,558
	Claudius	14	5,572
	Nero	13	5,585
110	Vespasian	10	5,595
	Titus	3	5,598
	Domitian	10	5,608
	Trajan	19	5,627
	Hadrian	21	5,648

115	Տիտոս	ի Դ	ՐՈՀԲ:
	Մարկոս	(ՃԲ)	ՐՃԱ:
	Կոմոդոս	ՃԴ	ՐՃԵ:
	Սեւերոս	ՃԹ	ՐՃԻԴ:
	Անտոնինոս	Է	ՐՃԼԱ:
120	Միլս Անտոնինոս	Դ	ՐՃԼԵ:
	Աղեքսանդր	ՃԴ	ՐՃԽԹ: /
222ա	Մաքսիմիանոս	Գ	ՐՃԾԲ:
	Գորգիանոս	Զ	ՐՃԾՃ:
	Փիլիպպոս	Զ	ՐՃԿԴ:
125	Դեկոս	Բ	ՐՃԿԶ:
	Գաղղոս	Գ	ՐՃԿԹ:
	Վաղերիանոս	ՃԵ	ՐՁՁԴ:
	Գաղիանոս	Բ	ՐՁՁՁ:
	Կղաւղէոս	Ա	ՐՁՁԷ:
130	Աւրեղիանոս	Զ	ՐՁՂԴ:
	Աւրինտիդոս	Ա	ՐՁՂԴ:
	Պոռոս	Է	ՐՊԱ:
	Կարառս	Բ	ՐՊԳ:
	Դիկոկղիտիանոս	իԲ	ՐՊԻ<Ե>:
135	Կոստանդիանոս	(իԲ)	ՐՊԾԷ:
	Նորին որդիքն	ի Դ	ՐՊՁԱ:

115	Titus	24	5,672
	Marcus	⟨12⟩	5,691
	Commodus	14	5,705
	Severus	19	5,724
	Antoninus	7	5,731
120	Another Antoninus	4	5,735
	Alexander	14	5,749
	Maximinus	3	5,752
	(Gordian)	6	5,758
	Phillip	6	5,764
125	Decius	2	5,766
	(Gallus)	3	5,769
	Valerian	15	5,784
	Gallienus	2	5,786
	Claudius	1	5,787
130	Aurelian	6	5,793
	Awrindiłos	1	5,794
	Probus	7	5,801
	Carus	2	5,803
	Diocletian	22	5,82(5)
135	Constantinus	⟨22⟩	5,857
	His son	24	5,881

Յուլլիանոս	Ա	ՌՊՁԲ:
Վաղէնտիոս	Է	ՌՊՁԹ:
Վաղէս	Ձ	ՌՊՂԵ:
140 Գրատիանոս	Ձ	ՌՋԱ:
Թէոթոս մեծ	ԺԵ	ՌՋԺԲ:
Նորին որդիքն	ԻԴ	ՌՋԽ:
Թէոդոս փոքր	ԼԷ	ՌՋՀԷ:
Մարկիանոս	Է	ՌՋՁԴ:
145 Զելոնդեանք	ԺԹ	ՑԹ:
Զենոն	ԺԲ	ՑԻԱ:
Անաստաս	(իե)	ՑԽԲ:
Յուստինիանոս	Թ	ՑԾԷ:
Իուստինոս	ԼԲ	ՑՂԵ:
150 Իուստինոս	ԺԱ	ՑՃԲ:
Տիբերեոս	Ձ	ՑՃՁԲ:
Մորիկոս	ի	ՑՃԼԲ:
Փաւկաս	Բ	ՑՃԽ:
Երակլիոս	Լ	ՑՃՀ:
155 Կոստանդինոս	Ա	ՑՃՀ(գ):
Կոստանդին	Բ	ՑՃՀԳ:

Լինին յԱդամայ մինչեւ ցայս վայր ամք ՑՃՀԳ:

Julian	1	5,882
Valentinian	7	5,889
Valens	6	5,895
140 Gratian	6	5,901
Theodosius the Great	15	5,916
His sons	24	5,940
Theodosius The Less	37	5,977
Marcian	7	5,984
145 The Leos	19	6,003
Zeno	18	6,021
Anastasius	⌜25⌝	6,048
Justinian	9	6,057
Justin	38	6,095
150 Justin	11	6,106
Tiberius	6	6,112
Maurice	20	6,132
Phocas	8	6,140
Heraclius	30	6,170
155 Constantinus	1	6,17⌜3⌝
Constans	2	6,173

These are 6,173 years from Adam up to this place.

ln 5   Arm has, literally Maɫaɫiel, a corrupted form
         of this name.

ln 7   MS has 1,295 for 1,297 arising from graphic
         error Ƅ for ƚ .

ln 13   Kainan: So LXX Gen 11:13, Luke 3:36.

ln 15   The reading for the name is unclear in the MS.

ln 17   MS has omitted final numeral, 7. There are two
         difficulties in the figures: If the total for
         Peleg is amended to 2,895, then between Peleg
         and Nahor there should have elapsed, by the
         totals, 241 years, but 132 + 130 + 79 produces
         341. Apparently an extra hundred years have
         entered at this point.

ln 20   For Isaac the totals imply a span of 166, opposed
         to the 60 offered.

ln 22   The total for Jacob implies a span of 80 or,
         alternatively the total should read 3,557.

ln 23   The total for Levi is corrupt and irretrievable
         on textual grounds. Extrapolating back from the
         coherent totals for Kohath and Amram, the total
         should be 3,605, but then the length of span for
         Levi should be the difference between 3,605 and
         either 3,552 or 3,557, i.e. 48 or 53.

ln 30   Addition off by one number.

ln 31   See Jud 3:7-11. Armenian reads a somewhat
         corrupt "K'usarsad".

ln 34   The MS reads "Awovk' and Amek". The first name
         is recognizably corrupt for the Armenian of
         "Ehud". The second is perhaps to be read as
         suggested here, cf. Jud 3:13.

ln 35   Abišu - the name apparently resembles Abishua the Levite, Phineas' son (1 Chr 6:4) - who was high priest after Phineas, so The Chronicle, p. 50 citing older sources. It is not, however, probable that a high priest is referred to here, and perhaps the name is related to "Jabin and Sisera".

ln 37   The second name is corrupted to "Zēt'" in the MS.

ln 40   The total for this line is off by one.

ln 47   Total corrupt, inner-Armenian for 4,293 or one year short in span.

ln 55   Apparently the number "1" has been lost following this total.

ln 56   The text reads "Abdiu", i.e. Obadiah, a corruption, cf. 1 Kings 15:2

ln 57   MS gives corrupt "Asaph".

ln 58   The span appears to be one off.

ln 62   The MS reads "Yozas".

ln 67   The totals or the spans for this plus the following lines are off: 4,758 + 29 = 4,777 (not 4,755) + 52 = 4,829 (or 4,827) not 4,832, which implies a span of 55 or 57.

ln 69   MS reads "Amos".

ln 75   The totals are off, 4,889 + 11 = 4,900 not 4,911.

ln 76   Apparently Neriglissar is referred to by this entry, which in the MS reads "Nirigłiat".

ln 86   The MS reads "Abedus".

ln 87   The MS reads "Awninas", cf. Jos. <u>Ant</u>. 5.2.7.

ln 89   The span of "14" is apparently corrupt for
           "12" - graphic.

ln 93   The span "7" is apparently corrupt for "24",
           perhaps by dittography from ln 95.

ln 96   Alcimus would be expected here. The name is
           not readily to be identified, but it may be
           corruption of "Jonathan". The order of events
           in the following lines is confused.

ln 100   Text reads "Hiwrkiasos".

ln 112   "Dometrianos" in the manuscript.

ln 114   "A n drianos" in the manuscript. Nerva is
           omitted, preceding Trajan.

ln 115   "Titus" is apparently corrupt for "Antonius
           Pius", perhaps by some sort of dittography
           from ln 111, <u>supra</u>.

ln 116   "12" is apparently corrupt for "19" by the not
           uncommon graphic confusion of ρ and θ.

ln 119   i.e. Caracalla, officially named M. Aurelius
           Antoninus.

ln 120   i.e. Elagabalus, who took the name M. Aurelius
           Antoninus

ln 123   MS has corrupt "Gorgian" by graphic error q/η.

ln 126   The MS has "Galdus" by graphic error η/η.

ln 131   This is apparently a corruption of some name,
           perhaps Florianus, but is not clear.

ln 134   The MS has 5,827, by graphic error b/ξ.

ln 135   The span "22" is apparently corrupt for "32"
           by dittography.

ln 139   The MS reads "Vałēs"

ln 145   The span of 25 is corrupt for 28 by graphic
          error ɥ/ɬ.

ln 148-149 The order of the names of Justin and Justin-
          ian should be reversed.

ln 155   The total is corrupt for 6,171.

NOTES

1 Ժամանակագրութիւն Տեառն Միքայէլի Ասորւոց Պատրիարքի
(The Chronicle of Lord Michael, Patriarch of the Syrians;
Jerusalem: St. James, 1871).

2 Cited according to J.-B. Chabot, Chronique de Michel le
Syrien (repr. Bruxelles: Culture et Civilisation, 1963)
15-17.

3 Cited according to C. Bezold, Die Schatzhöhle (Leip-
zig: Hinrichs, 1883-86). Bezold offers a Syriac text
and a German translation.

4 C.J.F. Dowsett(ed. and tr.) The History of the Caucas-
sian Albanians by Movses Dasxuranc'i (London: O.U.P.,
1961) 1-2.

5 B. Sarghissian, Անանուն Ժամանկագրութիւն (Anonymous
Chronicle; Venice: Mechitarists, 1904); the fullest
discussion is in the study by Markwart included in the
second edition of A. Bauer's edition of Hippolytus'
Chronicle (GCS 46; Berlin: Helm, 1955) 142-143.

6 Op., cit., p. xxv·

INDEX TO ONOMASTICA

Աբեղմայուղայ	Abełmayuła (s.v.)	I v A 25, C 15, D 14, E 11 F 22
Աբենէզեր	Abenēzer	I v A 23, B 48, C 18, D 12, E 12, F 21
Աբեննէր	Abennēr (s.v.)	I v A 22, B 45, C 17, D 5, E 13, F 20, III 18, V 11
Աբէսողոմ	Abēsołom (s.v.)	I v A 21, B 42, C 28, D 20, E 14, F 26, III 9, IV 12, V 12
Աբիա	Abia	I v D 21, E 16, III 10, V 13
Աբիաթար	Abiat'ar	I v A 20, B 37, C 26, D 18, E 15, F 28, III 11, V 14
Աբիան	Abian	VI i 5
Աբիգաղ	Abigal	III 13 app.
Աբիգայ	Abiga	III 13
Աբիգայիլ	Abigayil	III 12, V 15 comm.
Աբիգան	Abigan	I iv 20 app.
Աբիգեայ Աբիդա	Abigea (s.v.) Abida	I v A 19, B 39, C 27, F 29 I v D 19
Աբիդան	Abidan (s.v.)	I iv 20, v A 18, B 18, C 25, D 17, E 18, F 30
Աբիդաս	Abidas	III 5 app
Աբիդար	Abidar	I v B 19, D 18
Աբիդդար	Abiddar	I v A 24
Աբիդեա	Abidea	I v E 17
Աբիեսսեա	Abiessea	V 18
Աբիմեղեք	Abimełek' (s.v.)	I iv 11, v A 17, B 11, 13, C 24, D 16, E 19, F 31, III 14, IV 5, V 16, 79 app.
Աբինադաբ	Abinadab	III 15, V 17
Աբիոն	Abion	I v A 28, C 35, D 15, E 20, F 32
Աբիուդ	Abiud	I v A 37, C 37, D 23, E 21, F 33
Աբիուրիմ	Abiurim	I v A 35, C 36, D 22, E 22, F 34
Աբիսակ	Abisak	I v A 30, C 29, E 23, F 35, III 16, V 19
Աբներ	Abner	III 17 See Աբեննէր Abennēr

Աբոտ	Abot (s.v.)	I v C 39, D 24, E 24, F 36
Աբրաթ	Abrat'	I v A 32, D 28, E 26
Աբրահամ	Abraham (s.v.)	I iv 7, v A 15, 16, B 7, C 22, D 27, E 25, F 38, IV 45, V 21
Աբրայ	Abra (s.v.)	I v D 25, F 40, III 19, V 20, VI i 6
Աբրամ	Abram	I iv 6, v A 15, B 6, C 21, D 26, E 27, F 37, III 20, V 21 app., 22
Աբրոկ	Abrok	I v A 41, C 23, E 27a
Աբրոտ	Abrot	I v A 39
Ագաբ	Agab	V 23
Ագաբոս	Agabos (s.v.)	I v A 43, C 41, D 38, E 28, F 43, V 23 app.
Ագաբրամթովն	Agabŕamt'ovn	I v E 30
Ագագ	Agag	I iv 17, v A 41, 44, C 43, D 35, E 29, V 24, VI i 14.
Ագադ	Agad	I iv 17 app.
Ագաթանգեղոս	Agat'angełōs	I v D 31, VI i 10
Ագաթռեմովթ	Agat'ŕemovt' (s.v.)	I v D 33, VI i 11
Ագահ	Agah	V 23 app, VI i 9
Ագան	Agan	V 25
ագանել		I v D 34, VI i 13
Ագանովթայ	Aganovt'a	VI i 16
Ագապ	Agaṗ	I v D 30, VI i 8
Ագապէն	Agapēn	I v D 29, VI i 7
ագատութիւն		I v D 36, VI i 15
Ագար	Agar	I iv 8, v A 40, B 8, C 40, E 31, F 41, V 26
ագարակ		VI i 12
ագարակք		I v D 32
Ագարսա	Agarsa	I v D 37
Ագբակ	Agbak	IV 31

Ադոնիբեզեկ	Adonibezek	I iv 30, v A 4, B 24, C 7, E 40, F 3
Ադոնիզեբեկ	Adonizebek	See Ադոնիբեզեկ Adonibezek
Ադոնիէլ	Adoniēl	I v A 11, C 10, E 43, F 6
Ադոնիրամ	Adoniram	I v F 4
Ադոնմոյ	Adonmo	VI i 32
Ադովնայ	Adovna (s.v.)	I v A 8, C 8, E 41, F 5, IV 20, V 28, VI i 27
Ադովնիայ	Adovnia	I v A 9, C 9, E 42, F 7, IV 21, V 29 app., 30
Ադրաազար	Adraazar (s.v.)	I v A 6, C 12, E 44, F 12
Ադրամեղեք	Adrameɫek' (s.v.)	I v A 7, C 13, E 45, F 11, VI i 31 app.
Ազազայէլ	Azazayēl	I V E 46, F 47
Ազազիէլ	Azaziēl	IV 17
ազազուն		VI i 33
Ազայէլ	Azayēl	I v E 47, F 46
Ազան	Azan	I iv 31, v B 25, E 48, F 45
Ազապարայ	Azabara	I v E 49
Ազար	Azar	I v E 50, F 48
Ազարիայ	Azaria	I v F 49, IV 23, V 31,
ազգ		VI i 34
ազդեր		VI i 37
Ազդէովթ	Azdēovt'	VI i 38
ազդր		VI i 36
ազղող		VI i 35
Ազեկայ	Azeka	VI i 39
Ազմոլղեւ	Azmoldew	VI i 40
Ազոտոս	Azotos (s.v.)	I iv 37, v B 31, V 32
Ազդվր	Azdvr	V 33
Աթաղիա	At'aɫia	V 34

Ալելույիա	Aleluia (s.v.)	I v B 50, IV 15, V 38
Ալեփ	Alep'	I ii 1
Ակիտաբէլ	Akitabēl	See Ak'itop'el
Ակկարոն	Akkaron	I iv 39, v B 33, V 35
Ակրաբիմ	Akrabim	I iv 32, v B 26
Ահարովն	Aharovn (s.v.)	I iv 19, v B 17, IV 7, V 36
Ահովտ	Ahovt	V 37
Աղեկսանդէր	Aƚeksander	V 39
Աղեկսանդրիայ	Aƚeksandria	V 40
Ամաղեք	Amaƚek' (s.v.)	I iv 29, v B 23, IV 9, V 41
Ամամ	Amam	V 42
Աման	Aman	V 43
Ամանայ	Amana	V 44
Ամասիայ	Amasia	IV 30, V 47
Ամատտարա	Amattara	I v B 38
Ամարփադ	Amarp'aƚ	I iv 10, v B 10
Ամբակում	Ambakum	IV 28, V 45
Ամեսսաի	Amessai (s.v.)	I v B 47, V 47 app., 48
Ամէն	Amēn	IV 26, V 49
Ամէսիա	Amēsia	V 48 app.
Ամինադաբ	Aminadab	I iv 16, v B 15, IV 6, V 50
Ամմովն	Ammovn	I iv 12, v B 12, V 51
Ամնոն	Amnon	I iv 12 app., v 11, V 52, comm.
Ամոն	Amon	V 51 app., 52
Ամովս	Amovs	V 53, 54
Ամովսիայ	Amovsia	IV 16
Ամուրհացի	Amurhac'i	I iv 28, v B 22, IV· 8, V 55

Ամրամ	Amram	I iv 18, v B 16
Ամրի	Amri	V 46
Այենդովր	Ayendovr	I v B 41
Անաբովթ	Anabovt	See Անաթովթ Anat'ovt'
Անաթովթ	Anat'ovt'	I iv 33, v B 27, IV 10, V 57
Անանիայ	Anania	IV 22, V 56
Անգէաս	Angēas	V 58
Անգէ	Angē	V 58 comm.
անդրադարձումն		IV 41
Անդրիաս	Andrias (s.v.)	IV 25, V 59
անրնդ շատ		IV 37
Անթրակ	Ant'rak	I iv 25
Աննա	Anna	I iv 36, v B 30, IV 11, V 60
անուրջ		IV 36
անշրպետ		IV 38
Անտիոքիա	Antiok'ia	V 61
Անքուս	Ank'us	I v B 40
ապաշաւիլ		IV 40
Ապողոս	Apołos	V 62
Առած	Aṙac	I iv 23, IV 29
առ շաւատ շ եա		IV 39
Ասաել	Asael	I v B 46
Ասաթ	Asat'	I iv 15
Ասափ	Asap'	I v B 49
Ասեր	Aser	I iv 13, v B 13, V 63
Ասերովթ	Aserovt'	I iv 27 app., v B 19
Ասերովն	Aserovn	I iv 26 app., 27, v B 21

Աթթինէ	Ast'inē	V 64
Ասկալովն	Askalovn	I iv 38, v B 32, 33
Ասուր	Asur	I iv 5, v B 5, IV 19, V 65
Ասվերուս	Asverus	V 66
Աստարովթ	Astarovt'	V 67
Ասtին	Astin	I v B 50
Ասրովն	Asrovn	I iv 22
Ասքա	Ask'a	V 68
Արա	Ara	I v C 49
Արաբացիք	Arabac'ik'	V 69, 70
Արաբիա	Arabia	I v C 48
Արաբովթ	Arabovt'	I v A 45, C 45
Արամ	Aram	I iv 14, 18 app., v A 46, B 141, C 46, V 71
Արամաթի	Aramat'i	I v C 47
Արարատ	Ararat	V 72, 260
Արբոկ	Arbok	V 73
արզասաւոր		IV 33
արզաւանդ		IV 32
արդարեւ		IV 34
Արիմաթեմ	Arimat'em (s.v.)	I iv 40, v A 48, B 34, IV 13
Արիոպագոս	Ariopagos	V 74
Արիովն	Ariovn	I iv 26
Արիսպագոս	Arispagos	I v A 50
Արոն	Aron	I iv 22 app., V 75
արուարձան		IV 35
Արուէլ	Arūēl	I iv 34 app., v A 47, B 28
Արուէր	Aruēr	I iv 34, v B 28

Արտաքսերքսէս	Artak'serk'sēs	V 76
Արրա	Arra	I v C 50
Արփաքսաթ	Arp'ak'sat'	I iv 4, v A 44, B 4, C 44, IV 3, V 77
Արքեղաւոս	Ark'eławos	I v A 49
Աւգոստոս	Awgōstos	IV 24
Աւնան	Awnan	I iv 9, v B 9
Աւովդ	Awovd (s.v.)	I iv 35, v B 29
Ափփուսովթ	Ap'p'usovt'	I iv 24
Աքազ	Ak'az	IV 18, V 81
Աքայիա	Ak'ayia	V 80
Աքայեաբ	Akayeab	V 78
Աքարիմ	Λk'arim	I iv 21 app.
Աքերովք	Ak'erovk'	I v B 35
Աքիմաաս	Ak'imaas	I v B 44
Աքիմելեք	Ak'imelek'	I v B 36, V 79
Աքիտոփէլ	Ak'itop'el	I v B 43, IV 14, V 82
Աքիրամ	Ak'iram	I iv 21, v B 20
Աքուս	Ak'us	See Ank'us
Բաալ	Baal	VI ii 3
Բաաղ	Baał	VI ii 4
Բաաղիմ	Baałim	VI ii 5
Բաբայ	Baba	VI ii 1
Բաբելոն	Babelon	IV 42, VI ii 6
Բաբէլ	Babēl	V 83
Բաէլ	Baēl	VI ii 2
Բաթուէ	Bat'uē	V 84

Բաթուէլ	Bat'uēl (s.v.)	V 84, VI ii 7
Բաթ	Bat'	VI ii 8
Բալլա	Balla	V 86, 89
Բահաղ	Bahał	IV 55, V 85
Բաղաամ	Bałaam	V 87
Բաղակ	Bałak	V 88
Բաղտասար	Bałtasar	IV 50
Բանեա	Banea	V 90
Բաներեզէս	Banereg̅e̅s	V 91
Բառնաբաս	Bar̊nabas	IV 54, V 96
Բատոս	Batos	V 92
Բարակ	Barak	V 93
Բարդուղիմէոս	Bartułim̅e̅os	IV 51
Բարիովնա	Bariovna	V 94
Բարսաբայ	Barsaba	V 95
Բարուք	Baruk'	V 97
Բարտիմէոս	Bartim̅e̅os	V 98
Բեզեկ	Bezek	V 100
Բեթ	Bet'	I ii 2
Բեթանիա	Bet'ania	V 101
Բեթաբաթայ	Bet'abat'a	V 102
Բեթաւան	Bet'awan	V 103
Բեթդագոն	Bet'dagon	V 121
Բեթէլ	Bet'ēl	V 104
Բեթէր	Bet'e̅r	V 105
Բեթղէհեմ	Bet'le̅hem (s.v.)	IV 57, V 106
Բեթսաբէէ	Bet'sab̅e̅e̅	V 108
Բեթսաիդայ	Bet'saida (s.v.)	IV 44, 52, V 110
Բեթսամիւս	Bet'samiws	V 109
Բեթբաքէ	Bet'bak'e̅	V 111
Բեթբաքովր	Bet'bak'ovr	V 112
Բելա	Bela	V 123
Բելիար	Beliar	IV 46, V 113
Բելփեքովր	Belp'ek'ovr	V 114
Բեհմովթ	Behmovt'	V 115
Բեղզեբուղ	Bełzebuł (s.v.)	IV 53, V 99

Բենիամին	Beniamin	IV 43, V 116
Բենոնի	Benoni	V 117
Բեսելիէլ	Beseliēl	IV 48
Բետուլ	Betul	V 118
Բերա	Bera	V 119
Բերովբա	Berovba	IV 56
Բերսաբէ	Bersabē	IV 49, V 107, 110
Բէլ	Bēl	IV 45, V 122
Բէրէսիթ	Bērēsit'	V 126 app.
Բոյոս	Boyos	V 124
Բոսոր	Bosor	IV 47, V 125
Բրեսիթ	Bresit'	V 126
Գաբայա	Gabaya	V 127 app.
Գաբայադ	Gabayad	V 128
Գաբայեա	Gabayea	V 127
Գաբրիէլ	Gabriēl	V 129
Գադգադ	Gadgad	V 131
Գազեր	Gazer	V 132
Գաթ	Gat'	V 130
Գալաադ	Galaad	V 245 comm.
Գալիլեա	Galiea	V 133
Գալատացիք	Galatac'ik'	V 134
Գաղգաղայ	Gałgałay	V 135
Գաղգոթայ	Gałgot'a	V 143
Գեբաղ	Gebał	V 136
Գեդէոն	Gedēon	V 137
Գեհենին	Gehenin	V 139
Գեհոն	Gehon	V 138
Գերսոմ	Gersom	V 140
Գերսոն	Gerson	V 141
Գէթոն	Gēt'on	V 137 app.
Գոգ	Gog	V 142
Գոլմոր	Golmor	V 145 app.
Գողիաթ	Gołiat'	V 144
Գոմեր	Gomer	V 145
Գոմորայ	Gomora	V 146

Դաբրէիմովմին	Dabrēiovmin	V 147
Դագան	Dagan	V 148
Դաթան	Dat'an	V 150
Դալիա	Dalia	V 149 app.
Դալիլա	Dalila	V 149
Դաղեթ	Daɫet'	I ii 4
Դամասկոս	Damaskus	V 151
Դան	Dan	V 152
Դանիէլ	Daniēl	V 153
Դարեհ	Dareh	V 154
Դաւիթ	Dawit'	V 155
Դեբովրա	Debovra	V 156
Դիկապոլիս	Dekapōlis	V 157
Դիաբոլոս	Diabolos	V 158
Դիապոլոս	Diapolos	V 158 app.
Դիդիմոս	Didimos	V 159
Դիթալասոն	Dit'alason	V 160
Դինա	Dina	V 161
Դիոնիսիոս	Dionisios	V 162
Դովեկ	Dovek	V 163
Դովր	Dovr	V 164
Դովրա	Dovra	V 165
Եբաղ	Ebaɫ	V 166
Եբեր	Eber	V 167
Եբրայեցի	Ebrayec'i	V 168
Եգիպտոս	Egiptos	V 169
Եգղոմ	Egɫom	V 170
Եդեմ	Edem	V 171
Եդոմ	Edom	V 172
Եզեկիա	Ezekia	V 173
Եզեկիէլ	Ezekiēl	V 174
Եզրաս	Ezras	V 175
Եզրիէլ	Ezriēl	V 176
Եզրով	Ezrov	V 177
Եթամ	Et'am	V 178
Եթովպիա	Et'ovpia	V 179

Եղզանայ	Elgana	V 180	
Եղեքանան	Elek'anan	V 181 app.	
Եղքանան	Elk'anan	V 181	
Եկղեսիաստէս	Eklesiastēs	V 189	
Եղիա	Eɫia	V 182	
Եղազար	Eɫiazar	V 184	
Եղիակիմ	Eɫiakim	V 183	
Եղիմելէք	Eɫimelēk'	V 185	
Եղինաթան	Eɫinat'an	V 186	
Եղիշէ	Eɫišē	V 187	
Եղիսաբեթ	Eɫisabet'	V 188	
Եմաւուս	Emawus	V 190	
Եմմանուէլ	Emmanuēl	V 191	
Եյ	Ey		See Ec'
Ենգենիա	Engenia	V 192	
Եննոն	Ennon	V 193	
Ենովս	Enovs	V 194	
Ենովք	Enovk'	V 195	
Եսայիայ	Esayia	V 196	
Եսաւ	Esaw	V 197	
Եսթեր	Est'er	V 198	
Երեմէէլ	Eremēel	V 200	
Երեմիա	Eremia	V 201	
Երիքով	Erik'ov	V 202	
Երուսաղէմ	Erusaɫem	V 203	
Եւա	Ewa	V 204	
Եւբուլլոս	Ewbulos	V 199	
Եփրաթայ	Ep'rat'a	V 205	
Եփրայիմ	Ep'rayim	V 206	
Եփրոն	Ep'ron	V 207	
Եց	Ec'	I ii 16	
Զաբոն	Zabon	V 208 app.	
Զաբուղուն	Zabuɫun	V 208	
Զամրի	Zamri	V 209	
Զարայ	Zara	V 210	
Զաքարիայ	Zak'aria	V 211	

Կանա	Kana	V 241
Կասթին	Kast'in	v 242
Կարիաթարիմ	Kariat'arim	V 243
Կարիաթսեփէր	Kariat'sep'ēr	V 244
կարկառ		V 245
Կարմէլ	Karmēl	V 246
Կափառնայում	Kap'aṙnayum	V 247
Կեդար	Kedar	V 248
Կեդրոն	Kedron	V 249
Կերէաս	Kerēas	V 250
Կեփաս	Kep'as	V 251
Կինովթ	Kinovt'	V 252
Կիպրոս	Kipros	V 255
Կիս	Kis	V 253
Կիւրոս	Kiwros	V 256
Կղէոպաս	Kłēopas	V 254
Կողոսացիք	Kołosac'ik'	V 257
Կորբան	Korban	V 258
Կորխա	Korxa	V 259
Կոփ	Kop'	I ii 19
Հաբէղ	Habeł	III 7 app, See Abeł
Հայաստան	Hayastan	V 260
Հելի	Heli	V 262
Հելիպողիս	Helipołis	V 263
Հերմոն	Hermon	V 261
Հէ	Hē	I ii 5
Հնդիկք	Hndikk'	V 265
Հնդաստան	Hndstan	V 264
Հողեփենէս	Hołep'eṙnēs	V 266
Հռոմ	Hṙom	V 267
Հռութ	Hṙut'	V 268
Ղաբան	Łaban	V 269
Ղազարոս	Łazaros	V 270
Ղամեդ	Łamed	I ii 12
Ղամէք	Lamēk'	V 271
Ղապիովթ	Łapiovt'	V 272

Միսայէլ	Misayēl	V 312
Միսիա	Misia	V 310
Միքա	Mik'a	V 308
Միքայէլ	Mik'ayēl	V 309
Միքիա	Mik'ia	V 311
Մնէս	Mnēs	V 313
Մոգ	Moǧ	V 317
Մովաբ	Movab	V 314
Մովաս	Movas	V 315 app.
Մովսա	Movsa	V 315
Մովսէս	Movsēs	V 316
Յաբէթ	Yabēt'	V 323
Յակոբ	Yakob	V 318
Յամին	Yamin	V 319
Յայէլ	Yayēl	V 320
Յայիէլ	Yayiēl	V 321
Յասոն	Yason	V 322
Յեբուս	Yebus	V 324
Յեբուսթէ	Yebust'ē	V 326
Յեդովմէ	Yedovmē	V 355
Յեզոնիա	Yezonia	V 356
Յեմենի	Yemeni	V 327
Յեսբոք	Yesbōk	V 330
Յեսու	Yesu	V 332
Յեսսէ	Yessē	V 331
Յերապոլիս	Yerapōlis	V 325
Յերոբոադ	Yeroboał	V 333
Յերոբովամ	Yerobovam	V 334
Յեւայիմ	Yewayim	V 360
Յեփթայէ	Yep't'ayē	V 335
Յեքոնիա	Yek'onia	V 338
Յէու	Yēu	V 328
Յէուս	Yēus	V 329
Յիսուս	Yisus	V 336
Յոբ	Yob	V 339
Յոթորայ	Yot'ora	V 337

Յոյնք	Yoynk'	V 360
Յովաբ	Yovab	V 343
Յովակիմ	Yovakim	V 344
Յովաս	Yovas	V 345
Յովաքիմ	Yovak'im	V 346
Յովդ	Yovd	See C'ovd
Յովէլ	Yovel	V 347
Յովհաննէս	Yovhannēs	V 348
Յովնադաբ	Yovnadab	V 349
Յովնաթան	Yovnat'an	V 350
Յովնան	Yovnan	V 351
Յովսափատ	Yovsap'at	V 352
Յովսէփ	Yovsēp'	V 353
Յովսիա	Yovsia	V 354
Յովրամ	Yovram	V 357
Յորդանան	Yordanan	V 358
Յուդայ	Yuda	V 340
Յուլիոս	Yulios	V 341
Յունան	Yunan	V 342
Յքազ	Yok'az	V 359 app.
Յքաս	Yok'as	V 359
Նաբաթ	Nabat'	V 362, 383 app.
Նաբաղ	Nabał	V 363
Նաբովթ	Nabovt'	V 364
Նաբուգոդոնոսոր	Nabugodonosor	V 365
Նազարեթ	Nazaret'	V 366
Նազովրացիք	Nazovrac'ik'	V 367
Նաթան	Nat'an	V 368
Նաթանայէլ	Nat'anayēl	V 369
Նայասոն	Nayason	V 361
Նային	Nayin	V 369 app., 370
Նանթան	Nant'an	V 368 app.
Նաւում	Nawum	V 371
Նաքովր	Nak'ovr	V 372
Նեբրովթ	Nebrovt	V 375
Նեփթայիմ	Nep't'ayim	V 378

Նէապոլիս	Nēapōlis	V 374
Նէեման	Nēeman	V 373
Նէեմի	Nēemi	V 376
Նէովստան	Nēovstan	V 377
Նինուէ	Ninuē	V 379
Նոյ	Noy	V 380
Նոյոմին	Noyomin	V 381
Նուարեդդաբր	Nuareddabr	V 383
Նուն	Nun	I ii 14
Շաբաթ	Šabat'	V 383
Շին	Šin	I ii 21
Շուշանայ	Šušana	V 384
Ողողոմ	Odołom	V 385
Օզա	Oza	V 387
Օզիա	Ozia	V 388
Օզիէլ	Ôziēl	V 389
Ողա	Oła	V 390
Ողբադիայ	Ołbadia	V 392 app.
Օնէսիմէոս	Onēsimēos	V 386
Ոռնան	Ołnan	V 391
Ովբաթիա	Ovbat'ia	V 392
Ովբէթ	Ovbēt'	V 393
Ովնանայ	Ovnana	V 395
Ովսէէ	Ovsēē	V 396
Ովրէփ	Ovrēp'	V 397
Ովք	Ovk'	V 394
Որդիեկրայ	Ordiekra	V 398
Ուլա	Ula	V 387 app.
Ուրիա	Uria	V 399
Օքոզիա	Ok'ozia	V 400
Պաղիստինէ	Pałistinē	V 401
Պասեք	Pasek'	V 403
Պարասկեւէ	Paraskewē	V 402
Պենտէկոստ	Pentēkost	V 404
Պետրոս	Petros	V 405
Ջերոնիմոս	Jeronimos	V 406

Սեզորով	Segorov	V 442 app.
Սեդեկիա	Sedēkia	V 439
Սեդիմ	Sedim	V 440
Սելովամ	Selovam	V 451
Սելում	Selum	V 443
Սեհոն	Sehon	V 444
Սեղովմ	Sełovm	V 445
Սեմ	Sem	V 446
Սեմեի	Semei	V 447
Սենեքերիմ	Senēk'ērim	V 448
Սեփովրայ	Sep'ovray	V 450
Սէթ	Sēt'	V 441
Սէոն	Sēon	V 449
Սիբայ	Siba	V 452
Սիբողէթ	Sibołēt	V 453
Սիմէովն	Simēovn	V 454
Սիմոն	Simōn	V 455
Սին	Sim	V 456
Սինոյն	Sinoyn	C 457 app.
Սիոն	Sion	V 457
Սիսարայ	Sisara	V 458
Սիւքեմ	Siwk'em	V 459
Սիքոր	Sik'or	V 460
Սկարիովտացի	Skariovtac'i	V 461
Սոդոմ	Sodom	V 462
Սոմեր	Somer	V 463
Սովմնացի	Sov'mnac'i	V 464
Սորեկ	Sorek	V 465
Սոփիդիմ	Sop'idim	V 466
Ստեփաննոս	Step'annos	V 467
վաւ	Vaw	I ii 6
վաքաբովդ	Vak'abovd	V 468
Տարսոս	Tarsos	V 469
Տեթ	Tet'	I ii 9
Տիմէոս	Timēos	V 470
Տիմոթէոս	Timot'ēos	V 471

Տիտոս	Titos	V 472
Տիւրացիք	Tiwrac'ik'	V 473
Տուբիայ	Tubiay	V 474
Րեշ	Reš	I ii 20
Ցովդ	C'ovd	I ii 10
Փակեէ	P'akeē	V 475
Փաղեկ	P'ałek	V 484
Փանուէլ	P'anuēl	V 476
Փասկա	P'aska	V 477
Փարաւոն	P'arawon	V 478
Փարէզ	P'arez	V 479
Փարիսեցիք	P'arisec'ik'	V 480
Փենէշէզ	P'enēhēz	V 481
Փէ	P'ē	I ii 17
Փոքոր	P'ok'or	V 482
Փութ	P'ut'	V 483
Քաբ	K'ab	I ii 11
Քազբի	K'azbi	V 486
Քաղդեաստան	K'ałdēastan	V 485
Քաղէբ	K'ałēb	V 487
Քամ	K'am	V 488
Քամիլ	K'amil	I ii 3
Քանան	K'anan	V 489
Քեբրոն	K'ebron	V 490
Քետուրա	K'etura	V 491
Քոր	K'or	V 492
Քորազին	K'orazin	V 494
Քորեբ	K'oreb	V 493
Քուշ	K'uš	V 495
Քուս	K'us	V 496
Քրիստոս	K'ristos	V 497

GENERAL INDEX

This index does not include proper names of manuscripts included in the lists on pages xi-xvi and 212-217. Names included in the onomastic texts published are found in the preceding Onomastic Index.